MW00627694

Evolving with

SUBRAMANIAN SWAMY

a roller coaster ride

Evolving with SUBRAMANIAN SWAMY

a roller coaster ride

ROXNA SUBRAMANIAN SWAMY

ISBN: 978-93-5268-361-1

First Published 2017

Roxna Subramanian Swamy
A-77, Nizamuddin East
New Delhi - 110 013
INDIA
Mob: 9810834419
E-mail: roxnaswamy@gmail.com

Printed in India.

Contents

For Swamy's admirers, with my gratitude for their unstinted support; and to Lakshmi, who may or may not be an admirer but is certainly a well–wisher, who edited this book for me.

"----to thine own self be true;
And it must follow, as the night the day,
Thou canst not then be false to any man."
Shakespeare's "Hamlet".

PREFACE

The idea of this book arose just last July when someone in the BBC asked me for an interview about my life during the Emergency. I refused because after one or two experiences I am wary of the Media; but BBC persisted, so finally recollecting that during the Emergency there was one meeting with Atal Bihari Vajpayee, later Prime Minister of India, that I had never publicised (outside my family, I had told only Lal Krishna Advaniji of this meeting), I consented to be interviewed on the condition that the man would faithfully carry this recollection. He promised; and of course, he broke that promise. The broken promise confirmed my rather poor opinion of the time serving nature of the Indian Media/intelligentsia; and I realised that if this Vajpayee recollection was ever to go on record, it would have to be me who made the effort. The result is this book.

India is mind bogglingly huge and it is trite to say that there are many Indias. By birth and upbringing, Swamy fits into the India of the metropolises—he was brought up and lived for long periods and fought elections and organised political parties in giant metropolis Lok Sabha constituencies like New Delhi and Bombay North East; and he has also lived for considerable periods and organised and stood for elections in smaller cities like Madurai and Lucknow and Bhavnagar. But he knows that these do not provide the backbone of every all India political party; and so he has befriended the representatives of the rural constituencies and fitted into and toured these constituencies which ought to but do not always lay down the policies of government in Delhi. It is true that these gigantic rural constituencies, with their complicated caste loyalties and agricultural concerns, are not Swamy's natural habitat. That he empathises so strongly with them is the result of his deeply thought out views and commitments to what he calls the market economy and to traditional Hindu values. Socialism is "the s-word" for Swamy (though in the past decades, in Swamy's vocabulary it may be on the point of being replaced as a dirty word by that loathed misnomer, "secularism"); and you may imagine his delight when he discovered that in the 1950s, (this was before Swamy's time in politics) one of his icons, Chaudhary Charan Singh (who understood thoroughly and identified totally with the views and aspirations of the peasantry) had successfully shot down Jawaharlal Nehru's decision to collectivise agriculture on the Soviet model. As for me, I am city-bred and university-educated and grew up under the impression that India was a copybook democracy, that the administrative services and the police were there to maintain law and order and that in India the norms of civilised governance as enshrined in the Constitution, were a given. A life with Swamy may have opened my eyes to the glaring inadequacies of these beliefs.

To Swamy's admirers (they are who this book is written for), I must emphasize that though I have a deep faith in and admiration of Swamy, it stops short of aspiring to any particular post/designation/destination for him. I emphasize this here at the outset, only because sometime mid last year, a particularly hysterical anti-Swamy campaign appeared in the Media: its purpose apparently to warn a friend, the present Prime Minister, that Swamy had an eye on his job! And it was backed up by—of all things!—an old quote from me. Some years ago, I had been interviewed by some Press man and been asked whether I thought Swamy would make a good Prime Minister. All I replied truthfully (if I am quoted aright) was: "He's brilliant no doubt. Because he's so brilliant, people want to put him down. Even now he's capable of being Prime Minister." I must emphasize that I did not imply/prophesy that Swamy *would* be Prime Minister (that of course, has always been in the lap of the gods): only that, if despite the baleful efforts of the many insecure and green-eyed, he is called on, Swamy would make a good Prime Minister! All I can actually guarantee is that Swamy will always be true to himself.

Chapter I

THE PRECURSOR TO SWAMY: DADDY

I

This is really a book about Swamy, and to a much lesser extent, about me; but I could not have learnt to love, respect and value him as much as I do had I been brought up by someone other than my beloved father. So, I think it is appropriate to begin with a small account of Daddy and my days under his conservative and very disciplined tutelage.

By nature I am a law abiding person,—the question is: is it by nature, or simply because I grew up thinking that the law in India was developed in a universally accepted civilised way for "people like us"....it must have had something to do with my father. Never as far as I can recall, had Daddy, the most unassuming martinet in his private life, ever put on side or let us feel we could ever have access to any privilege....indeed for many years as children we did not even realise that in fact he was a very privileged person, a member of the I.C.S. (the Indian Civil Service) whose word no doubt was deemed the LAW to large swathes of Indian society (and certainly to the Police

–whether officers or humble constables) and with the power to get all sorts of Governmental things done through his mastery of the art of footnoting, and brief notes appended no doubt with his small and extremely neat, clear and decisive handwriting and signature, citing chapter and verse.

In fact for the first decade of our existence, my siblings and I didn't quite know what exactly Daddy did for a living: when as a ten year old, I was shifted from Delhi to Bombay and I joined a new school, a curious fellow student asked me what my father did, I said he was a secretary; and probably like me my school friend must have assumed that Daddy sat at a desk with a shorthand book, typing away for dear life…this particular friend was quite as clueless as I about rank in society, because on my return query she told us her father was, "a general"…so I visualised someone in khaki uniform and epaulettes leading batches of soldiers…it was only much later that I learnt that this particular gentleman was in fact, "Accountant General of Bombay" with absolutely no military credentials, and that my father, far from being a member of some steno pool, was in fact Secretary to the Bombay Government.

The revelation really dawned on us at the end of my school days, only after Daddy was transferred from Bombay to Ahmadabad. In direct contrast to the experience of the tin god from the Mofussil, who had been adulated in the Provinces – only to get his come-uppance when he had arrived in Rome to find that here he was nothing compared to the marble gods of Rome, we found that my unassuming father was now a VIP marble God, the Commissioner of Gujarat. I believe it was a case of being kicked upstairs, because there was a not very cordial connection with his Ministers in Bombay: we had a Congress Government in place in Bombay and its Ministers probably did not appreciate Daddy's firm and very definite notes explaining, with chapter and verse and a thorough knowledge of the laws and by-laws and notifications, that something the Hon'ble Minister wanted, could simply not be done.

So there was Daddy in Gujarat. We lived in Ahmadabad in an ancient monument which had started life as Shah Jahan's palace when he was Governor of Gujarat; and which after the British overran Gujarat, had been "modernised" by the simple expedient of building rooms and bathrooms and connecting corridors on top of the Mughal terraces. These were done in simple late nineteenth century British Raj style and made no attempt to fit in with the Mughal arches, niches and mouldings that Shah Jahan had favoured. And their authenticity was not really improved by successive Commissioner's wives who spent a small fortune in giving themselves some privacy by adding frilly chintz curtains to the huge Mughal darbar door arches (you just inserted industrial age wall brackets and curtain rods into the ancient stone and chunam walls; but there was no way you could make your early twentieth century sofa-sets or the glass topped fitted office furniture of the mid twentieth century look at all at home in a durbar hall that should have housed at least a peacock throne: our family's own unique contribution was to put a table tennis table in one of the side durbar halls). Nor was the monument really protected by the PWD, no one not brought up in government services really knows what the PWD (the Public Works Department) is; but we inheritors of the Raj, grew up thinking that any problem, from a leaking tap to a malfunctioning fridge to a clogged drain to a broken wall or ceiling, could be solved by calling up the PWD which obligingly sent across a mason every time an ancient wall or terrace or ceiling needed plastering down or over. The Archaeological Survey of India must have attempted some sort of control on the building because they had put up a few Curzon era notices threatening with a fine of "up to two hundred rupees", if one did "any act which causes or is likely to cause damage or injury to any part of the monument"; but though we children read and re-read all these notices with interest and discussed threadbare the huge two hundred rupee limit, (it has now been increased to five thousand rupees) we—like the officers, the Commissioners' wives and the PWD—lived with these threats without any particular attempt to mend our ways. It was not till more than half a century later, in the second decade of the twenty-first century when a vengeful Congress Central Government attempted to overnight demolish the top floor of our Nizamuddin home in Delhi, did I really study the various Ancient Monuments and Archaeological Sites and Remains Acts to understand their lethal potential and to discover with great delight, how much thought had gone into them and indeed how many glaring holes there were in that legislation and its successors.

Daddy, not being a style purist or particularly archaeologically correct, was happy enough with this palatial Office-cum-residence in Ahmadabad which he could run untroubled largely by Ministerial interference; but really he was like a pig in clover when he could get out in the districts "on tour", visiting his beloved villages and small towns which no doubt he had administered several decades earlier as a humble Collector Sahib and District Judge. Sometimes he would take us with him and we discovered to our awe, that when Daddy's car arrived in some back-of-beyond village, a posse of half a dozen policemen would line up and present arms. Admittedly the arms were probably of the 1860 Mauser vintage, nothing as lethal as the concealed revolvers and Uzies carried by Swamy's PSO's and the jeep load of policemen that have been inflicted on us almost continuously since the 1990's —they were stopped only during Atal Bihari Vajpayee's regime; and resumed after he demitted office, so you might see a connection—; and Daddy would courteously respond; but internally he was probably kicking himself for having to go through this rigmarole and salute back. And when Daddy left again there would be that presentation of Mausers to see him off.

Fifty years later when I went through Gujarat with friends, one of whom was herself the wife of a retired Secretary to the Government of India, and who of course had started life in the Districts as the Memsahib of Collector Sahib and Magistrate Sahib, she told me indignantly, "Roxna, that sort of thing went out with the British!"....but she was wrong: only a few months ago, I accompanied Swamy, an established politician whom the Gorkhas of the Darjeeling Hill Districts Administration wanted to make much of; and sure enough the Mauser wielding Policemen were there lined up to salute Swamy…. India does not change that fast.

After such a heady introduction to the members of the police (the only minions of the law we actually came in contact with at that age), it was impossible for us to conceive that the Police was anything but a humble and law abiding Servant of the People, there to make sure we were properly looked after. It took Swamy and the Emergency to shake that perception.

II

Under a gruff and authoritarian exterior, my father was a very shy and private person. So one did not readily discover how deep and brilliant those still waters ran. For instance, it was only from my mother that I learnt that at the University of Cambridge he had emerged as the Senior Wrangler of his year. She, poor lady, frankly confessed her ignorance of all things mathematical outside of her household accounts which she maintained with puritanical thoroughness; but from our earliest years I can remember that Daddy's idea of relaxation was to stretch out on his planter's chair and work away at some abstract mathematical idea. And please note, that to Daddy Mathematics was not arithmetic or even algebra or calculus but Relativity and Quantum Mechanics to which he added a dash of Astronomy and rather surprisingly Astrology... Mathematics must run in the genes of both Swamy and me: my grandfather and my father-in-law both taught Mathematics at the University level; and both Swamy and I did our Bachelors' degrees in Mathematics; one daughter and her husband graduated in electrical engineering from IIT Kanpur before moving on to do research and teach in the U.S.; and my second daughter graduated with a degree in Statistics; and our granddaughters (both Indian and American) have a splendid record in High School Maths including Math Olympiads—sometimes putting to shame both Swamy and me, whose mathematics is now rusty with dis-use.

Daddy had been brought up to be frugal with paper; so all his thoughts on Mathematics were compressed between the lines of the Company Share Reports which he collected and collated to the point that eventually he made quite a large fortune investing in the Share Market. I now regret that no one (including Daddy himself), thought to preserve and study those notes on mathematics made between the lines of old Company Share Reports: human knowledge might well have been expanded to brilliant and innovative mathematical concepts such as those he developed later in his only book, "The Evolution of Mattera".

Also he was painfully shy of exhibiting his expertise. I can remember one vignette as a teenager. We were staying as guests to some Maharaja, who was entertaining him in his Commissioner of Gujarat avatar. Once our host learnt that Daddy had studied mathematics, he waxed eloquent on some theory of his own on how to remember the multiplication table; and Daddy listened to him politely without letting on that his own mathematical expertise was in rather more rarified areas.

Similiarly, as a child I had little idea that he was a dab at languages: when after Independence, the then Chief

Minister of Bombay State, Morarjibhai Desai insisted that all senior civil servants pick up some literacy in the national language Hindi, I believe Daddy floored all his groaning colleagues by whizzing through all the Hindi language exam papers. I knew he had a knowledge of Persian only because he once casually told me that at the Cambridge Entrance Exams which then required a knowledge of Latin, he was permitted to offer Avesta in place of Latin. For a very short time in his early ICS career, he was posted in Belgaum and Dharwad and he emerged with a fluent knowledge of what he called, "Canarese" (and what less Anglicised persons now know as Kannada). He knew Sindhi, because like many Parsi officers, he had been posted in Sindh for some years, (they were perceived to be even-handed between Hindus and Muslims there). He spoke Marathi because that was the language around him most of his life (his parents settled in Poona and his wife's family had been settled there for two hundred years). And unlike us younger generation, he was fluent in his mother tongue Gujarati.

III

Recently, after all the hullaballoo about the defence helicopter misappropriated in Goa, by some Minister's kin, I remembered a little known story about Jawaharlal Nehru and his attitude towards the Nation's Property—and my father's role therein.

It was in the early fifties; and there were floods in Bihar. An American journalist interviewing Nehru, apparently expressed a wish to view the floods from the air; and Nehru, always with a glad eye for a comely white woman, assured her he would make her wish come true.

Accordingly, he directed the Defence Ministry to make a plane available for the lady. The file came to my father, then a lowly Joint Secretary in the Ministry of Defence, with a proper respect for the Nation's property, a contempt for Nehru's well known lady-killer propensities and a deep respect for Sardar Patel who had not only been his Minister but had also shared with him a feeling for the Sardar's hometown Nadiad, where my father had once been District Judge.

A stickler for the Rule Book, my father turned down the oral requisition of a Defence Plane. M.O. Mathai, Nehru's private secretary called my father in, to point out to him that this was the wish of the mighty Prime Minister himself. " Nehru has no authority to requisition a defence plane for this purpose", said my father; and when Mathai persisted, my father(using what every seasoned bureaucrat knows is the ultimate Sudershan Chakra, to be used only at your peril) told him, "Give it to me in writing". Mathai went and reported this to Jawaharlal Nehru.

An indignant Nehru hauled up my father's senior Mr. H. M. Patel, and demanded to know who had had the temerity to cross his wishes and directed that the errant civil servant be hauled up before him. With some trepidation, "H.M." told my father, warning him that Nehru was in the mood for blood. Accordingly my father presented himself before Nehru, who gave him a long lecture on India and freedom and accused my father, "You people still think you are working under the British". He then demanded that my father sign the requisition. (Some seventy years later, one may well wonder what exactly Mr. Nehru thought that people did, "working under the British". Was it acceptable in free India, to commandeer an air force plane to oblige a friend though it would not have been permitted "under the British"?)

"Give it to me in writing", repeated my father. Whereupon, Nehru treated him to a further flood of words, of which the most prominent and least offensive was the epithet "hide bound bureaucrat". Nehru then directed my father once more to release the plane. Once more my father repeated, "Give it to me in writing."—But Nehru did not give his order in writing, my father did not sign the requisition, no doubt the lady was disappointed; and my father was sent off to the boon docks. Well not exactly the boon docks; merely back to Bombay with a reputation for being "difficult".

My taciturn father did not circulate the story, though of course his colleagues got to hear of it because there had been witnesses. But when years later, hearing of it from my mother, I questioned him, he told it to me, adding with a reminiscient twinkle, " He kept calling me a HIDE BOUND BUREAUCRAT!" I am sure Daddy thought it was a compliment.

IV

Years later, after he had resigned from the service and taken up a rather lucrative job as a "boxwallah", Daddy had a second tussle with Nehru. He needed the company job: he had resigned in some haste when he was superceded and passed over from becoming Chief Secretary of Gujarat State, and, since he had not prepared well in advance for retirement, all he had was his savings (albeit these were quite large simply because he had trained his family to be frugal), a provident fund and a rather meagre pension(I think it worked out to something like five thousand rupees a year); and he had four children to be put through college. But an indignant Nehru waxed eloquent in Parliament on greedy civil servants influencing industrialists to give them jobs after retirement. There was very little he could do against my father who had already resigned and retired; but, by getting Parliament to pass a law on the subject, Nehru ensured that future retiring bureaucrats should not be able to get another job for some years after they retired. Thus in a way, Daddy was responsible for the "cooling off period" concept that today is very much a part of the civil servant's terms of service.

He crossed views with the Government over bank nationalisation also. It is true that a lot of his savings were invested in bank shares; but that is not why he supported the lawyers who spearheaded the bank nationalisation case, R.C. Cooper Vs. Union of India. For him private property was a way of life, rightly put among the fundamental rights in the Constitution; and the Supreme Court's striking down of the nationalisation, was for him a vindication that India was headed in the right direction. In that he turned out to be at one with his future son-in-law.

Daddy took on his last tussle with the Government in the 1960s and 1970s, by which time actually, between his investments in the share market and his earnings as a boxwallah, he had become quite wealthy; so he did not really need the five thousand rupee annual pension which formed the basis of his fresh claim against the Government of India. He lost eventually; but only after he had the singular distinction of forcing the Parliament of the day to amend the Constitution of India.

Daddy knew the law because he had studied it at Lincolns Inn; and worked thereafter as a District Judge for some years. So he knew that to safeguard the service conditions of ICS officers, the framers of the Constitution of India had included therein Article 314, which guaranteed to every person appointed by the Secretary of State in Council, (i.e. all ICS officers) the same conditions of service as that person was entitled to immediately before the commencement of the Constitution. Among other conditions, this included the right to a pension of 1000 pounds per annum or its equivalent in rupees at the rate of one shilling and six pence to the rupee. As I pointed out, this originally amounted to something like rupees five thousand per annum; but some time in the 1960s the rupee was devalued; and my "hidebound" father calculated that his 1000 pounds per annum pension had to be proportionately increased to earn him the princely sum of Rs. 13,333/- per annum; and when the Government of India turned down his demand, Daddy went to the Gujarat High Court in a Writ Petition. In 1971, faced with the clear terms of Article 314, the High Court had no option but to allow Daddy's Writ Petition and to declare him entitled to the enhanced pension. It would not have broken the back of the Indian economy; but of course the powers that be could not allow him to get away with that. Parliament amended the Constitution and deleted Article 314. With the protection of Article 314 gone, and a new Act—the Former Secretary of State Service Officers (Conditions of Service)Act 1972—in place the Government had no difficulty in getting the Supreme Court to reduce Daddy's pension to its original Rs. 5000 per annum, (It is a judgment reported in AIR(1974)SC 2055). By then Daddy was really quite wealthy and I don't think the humble pension amount made any great inroads into his style of living; but the hidebound bureaucrat felt satisfied that he had made his point.

V

I really regret now that I never followed up on his work as an ICS officer (perhaps we were just too young and Daddy just too taciturn to tell us); but I do know he was much respected by his colleagues. And I am told he did a good job. Years later when Swamy as a Member of Parliament would introduce me to any of the senior Congress ministers from Maharashtra, they invariably spoke to me of their respect and appreciation of Daddy's work.

Daddy though just, could be quite merciless, to both his underlings and also his children. You may recall that Mark Twain in "Following the Equator", once exclaimed, "I wish I was a chaprasi." Outside of a few High Courts and recently the Supreme Court (till Balakrishnan.C.J. got struck by the magnificence of the chopdars of the Bombay High Court, Supreme Court peons wore just a simple grey outfit of bush shirt and pant), the pattawala or chaprasi no longer exists in the services; but when we were children in the last days of the Raj and the early days of Independance, they were as ubiquitious as the Army batmen. They were definitely not the "peons" that abound today, who not only can read the files they carry around but actually use their access to them to squeeze something out of the hopeful or hapless subject of the file. In the first place they were called "pattawalas" simply because they wore a "patta": a black leather belt which looped from the shoulder to the waist and had on it a large oval brass replica of the Government Seal. Originally they wore turbans; and the uniform had scarlet and gold overtones (which was the genesis of Mark Twain's envy); but after Independence, in deference to the new Regime, they were put into white khadi kurta pajamas, the "patta" and a Gandhi topi.

You would be puzzled to work out what work exactly these pattawalas did. I suspect that they themselves were not quite sure of their place in the bureaucracy: possibly simple country lads lucky enough to have got appointed (through the influence of some Officer's domestic servant) to a sinecure for life. Most of them just sat outside the Officer's home and watched the world go by. Perhaps they were intended to act as a showpiece indicating the importance of the Officer they were attached to, like the Guards outside Buckingham Palace. And if my father had not dealt ruthlessly with the pretensions of one such pattawala posted outside our house, I would also have assumed that that was all they were there for.

I now remember with sympathy this particular pathetic pattawala. He used to sit day after day on a Government issue stool outside our front door, doing nothing, thereby fueling the simmering indignation of my busybody mother. For people like my mother who saw him hanging around the front of the house sitting on a stool and doing precisely nothing the livelong day, it seemed a waste of man power; so eventually she gave into her indignant instincts, handed him a duster and directed him to dust the family books. He objected. My mother brought it to the notice of Daddy; who called him in and asked him just what he was prepared to do. If the truth were told, he would have said that his job was purely ornamental: to hang out in front of the house and add to the dignity of the Secretary Sahib; but when pressed he stated that his job was to carry files and office letters from the Secretary Sahib to other Government functionaries.

So Daddy handed him a letter addressed to some Government functionary in Kurla, a good twenty miles away and told him to go and deliver it and return. "What about my bus fare?" he asked. But Daddy stated that he knew of no rule entitling him to any such amount. And so the poor crestfallen man was not even given the bus fare to Kurla....I cannot remember what happened to him. But it did tell me how ruthlessly Daddy and the ICS could deal with the recalcitrant underling in the days before the Unions came into existence.

Years later when I told Swamy the incident, he was very disapproving. It proved, he said, that what Daddy lacked was "vivek": a very Indian expression that suggests discrimination and the ability to make due adjustment. It may surprise Swamy's numerous critics; but really he is a very reasonable and adjusting person, whose friendly frankness has managed to make and keep friends and allies across the whole convoluted spectrum of Indian politics. How often have I met some diehard Communist Member of Parliament who has confessed that on getting to know Swamy (reputed in their inner conclaves to be some sort of being with horns and a tail) they had found a reasonable and open minded human with whom they could discourse and disagree civilly. The only thing Swamy will not tolerate is insincerity, backstabbing and backdoor intrigue, which unfortunately is often the stuff of getting ahead in all political parties.

Chapter II

SWAMY'S EARLY YEARS

I

Well that was in the 1940s and the 1950's before Subramanian Swamy made his appearance and messed up all the comfort and certainty of my earlier life and beliefs. I met and married Swamy in the U.S.: we were both graduate students at Harvard University; but I must humbly confess, there the resemblance ended. I was in the School of Engineering and Applied Mathematics, an excellent school with the normal quota of brilliant professors and faculty, including Nobel laureates but not quite the scope and breadth of the stars in the engineering field (that honour was shared in my days, by M.I.T., "that trade school across the Charles", and Berkeley at the other end of the American continent); and there I struggled to maintain some sort of standing. Swamy on the other hand was enrolled in the Harvard University School of Economics, a name to conjure with in all corners of the globe; and even among their very brilliant students, he shone.

In the first place even his admission there was unusual. Swamy was generally considered in his immediate family as the rather ordinary if not actually dumb one of the brood. They were five children: the brilliant dynamic eldest sister Vatsala intended to go into politics and social service and literature all at once, the quiet scholarly second one Sushila was slated to be a doctor (though eventually she ended up as a librarian because she fainted at her first dissection class), then Swamy, then Nirmala, shy and pretty. Unfortunately as a child Nirmala contracted polio and developed a stiff arm and leg: when she went back to school as a seven or eight year old, some cruel child laughed at her so she returned home in tears, my father-in-law took her out of school and she did not really get any school education after that. She really was as bright and gifted (indeed quite as sharp tongued) as any of the others and she was always treated tenderly (till today Swamy gets a rakhi every year from her and responds with love) but as if she had neither ability or responsibility; so people who did not know the family well, assumed she must be retarded. Finally there was a younger son, Ram. Swamy was dismissed as the easy going loafer, a vagabond because of his uncaring-of-consequences attitude to life, who excelled in cricket and swimming and playing with his beloved dog Winnie and was not expected to amount to much. That is, he was dismissed in that way by his father and siblings, but not his mother, who always had a deep, touching and abiding faith in his capacity and sincerity… Swamy still remembers with emotion, how she saved from her housekeeping money to get him his first wristwatch.

Of course it was expected that he would have to earn a livelihood; and he was considered lucky to have his uncle's contacts: his uncle Ramakrishnan, had by brains, application and hard work risen to high rank in the boxwallah company, Imperial Tobacco, and he secured an entrée for Swamy in a "covenanted" post in Imperial Tobacco. But at the interview, Swamy fluffed this career in a rather unusual but typically Swamy fashion. Probably to check out his table manners, Ramakrishnan's boss took them out for lunch. After lunch the boss pulled out a cigarette and put it to his lips. Ramakrishnan nudged Swamy: it was the signal that Swamy should light the cigarette; but Swamy the proud had never done anything so subservient as light someone else's cigarette and he refused to do that and so walked out of consideration for the proposed "covenanted" job….. after that my father-in-law could only suggest that Swamy try for a job as apprentice foreman in the Bhilai steel plant or perhaps in the lower rungs of the Army……No one in the family seems to have realised or nurtured Swamy's brilliance and independence, which is strange because at his school leaving exam and in College he topped in Mathematics.

II

Swamy's father, Subramanian was himself a brilliant Mathematics student in the best "Madrasi Brahmin " tradition. Unusually (Swamy's bloodlines are pure Iyer Brahmin) his family was actually a land-owning one who lorded it over the village of Mullipallam near Sholavandan in the Dindigul District to the north of Madurai. My father-in-law liked to leave people with the impression that as a boy he spent his days herding the village cows on the banks of the Vaigai; but since he went on to study at the rather elite St. Joseph's College in Trichinopoly and later Annamalai University, I expect that was not quite accurate.

Brahmins in Tamil Nadu, are not usually wealthy or land owning, but Swamy's family were descendants of Ramappaiya Iyer, who used to be Commander in Chief (Dalavay) of the seventeenth century Madurai monarch Tirumala Nayak. The history books that I have managed to cull, are not quite clear as to Ramappaiya Iyer's role in history and whether it was a good thing or not. Tirumala Nayak is best remembered for the magnificent monuments he constructed, including his still extant Palace in Madurai and parts of the Meenakshi Temple there. All that cost money; and, in the best later Swamy mode, apparently Ramappaiya Iyer made himself unpopular with the ruler by trying to police his expenditure; so although he was credited with a victory against a Mysore Army (then under orders from the Vijaynagar Emperor), which had reached as far as Dindigul, the king ordered him to retire to his lands in Mullipallam. (I don't read Tamil, so I have not gone to original Tamil sources, and I am reduced to quoting a book printed by Higginbotham in 1913, which says of the matter:

> "When the news of the invasion reached the ears of Tirumala, he hastily mustered his forces and dispatched them under his able general Ramappaiya, who rallied round him the panic stricken poligars of Dindigul and turned the tables on the enemy by

> carrying the war into Mysore. There he laid siege to the capital. But in the very hour of victory he had peremptory orders from Tirumala who had allowed his ears to be poisoned by a court faction against the minister. Like Nelson in the famous battle of the Baltic, the resourceful Dalavay rose equal to the occasion, pretended ignorance of the order until the enemy surrendered and then hastened to the capital with such a formidable force and surrounded by a body of faithful poligars that Tirumala thought it wise to change his attitude immediately and welcome the victorious general with honours and rewards. The Mysore war was thus abandoned when a profitable peace might have been concluded; the loyalty of an able general was tampered with while his services were still required by the State.")

Later when he was needed for a further campaign against Ramnad, Ramappaiya Iyer was recalled by Tirumala; but this time while constructing a causeway to cross the channel separating Rameswaram from the mainland, Ramappaiya Iyer died suddenly. Swamy never cared to absorb all the above information about his forbear; it might have taught him something about how to handle the political powers that be today.

Ramappaiya Iyer's descendants continued to farm their lands in Mullipallam until the days of my father-in-law's father Sitarama Iyer. Unfortunately Sitarama was of a litigative nature; and seems to have lost lawsuit after lawsuit. He was forced to sell all his lands and even his house was sold by the British administrators to recover taxes. My father-in-law took no interest in the matter and despite his wealthier brother's later attempts at repossession, the house was not recovered until some dozen years ago, when the mortgage was paid off by Swamy himself, who thus got possession of his ancestral home.

Swamy is not in the least sentimental or artistic and has little use for a heritage home. The house, which I saw only once in 1969, on a trip, was a rather lovely typical South Indian agraharam bungalow: external sit out verandah, middle courtyard, shining red oxide tiled floors, swings in the courtyard which was surrounded by the living quarters; but it had no indoor lavatory. So, I discovered (too late!) to my horror, the practical Swamy had it bulldozed down and replaced by a tasteless featureless but waterproof modern house with plumbing and toilets. There is a caretaker and Swamy visits it about once in a decade. I believe, under pressure from our dear friend Lakshmi Nalapat, the house was most recently occupied by a group of Kerala priests who were set to remove any bad vibes that may have collected since Ramappaiya Iyer's days.

III

But to get back to my father-in-law, Sitarama Subramanian was an idealist and a freedom fighter, who signalled his belief in Mahatma Gandhi's anti-caste movement, by dropping his revealing surname Iyer.—which is why now Swamy's full name is Subramanian Swamy and nothing more. Later in a further affirmation of his disbelief in the caste system, my father-in-law refused to perform any thread ceremony for his children, so I suppose that strictly speaking

Swamy is not even a twice born Brahmin. He taught for some time at Annamalai University; but when he was offered a Government job in Delhi as Statistician to the British officer Sir Theodore Gregory who was Economic Adviser to the Government of India, he felt he owed it to his growing family (at that time there were only the two daughters Vatsala and Sushila), to accept. So the family moved to Delhi with the occasional stationing in the summer capital of Simla. So though Swamy was born in Madras, he was promptly shifted to Delhi and though the family visited its relations in Tamil Nadu during vacations, he grew up in Delhi. Years later, a puzzled Chaudhary Charan Singh who could not understand how a "Madrasi" had developed Swamy's belligerent Jat-like propensities, finally concluded that the Delhi up-bringing explained it all: obviously the Chaudhary did not have much experience with the proud Tamil heritage of belligerence and military prowess –the Pallavas and the Cholas *did* conquer much of South East Asia—and could only draw on his personal experience with the stereotypical meek Delhi-based Tamil typist.

My father-in-law and Swamy did not get on well; but he gave him a value system that anyone could be proud of. He never cared deeply about money or property or even clothes: in an era when bureaucrats in Delhi showed off their suits and boots and foreign garments, and even fairly simple people like my father looked askance at people in "native" garb, he continued wearing his dhotis and khadis and chappals with pride and dignity. Left to himself he would not even have bought a house for his retirement days, saying he could always rent; but he did so to satisfy my mother-in-law. But even that purchase was typical of him. Like many senior Government officers of his generation, he had been allotted a subsidised plot of land in the Delhi bureaucrats' dream colony then coming up, Vasant Vihar. Later my father-in-law decided he was going to settle after retirement not in Delhi but in Bangalore; so he wrote to the Government surrendering his Vasant Vihar allotment....Today a Vasant Vihar house is worth its weight in gold and I think some other members of his family never forgave him for such fecklessness; but Swamy at least cannot be accused of having ever reproached him for such unworldliness. On the contrary, Swamy has a firm conviction that you do not collect the goods of this world: when you want something, that should be solely to increase your efficiency and effectiveness; and then you simply stretch out your hand (Brahmin-Beggar fashion) and the heavens drop the desired object (a scholarship, a basket of fruit, a dinner at the Taj or yet another mobile phone) in your hand. So—a great disadvantage for a politician—he has never felt the need to be corrupt.

Lest some cynical reader feels that the above analysis of Swamy's philosophy is unbelievably pious, in Chapter VII hereafter, I give a few significant instances of how this principle has worked in Swamy's life.

To get back to Swamy's childhood, apart from the continual fracas with a rather overbearing father, Swamy seems to have had a very normal childhood: a control freak, my father-in-law lavished most of his concern and pride on his brilliant eldest daughter and youngest son, continually holding them up as examples to Swamy, considered the duffer of the clan. Since Swamy, typically, is someone who has never allowed himself to be ordered around, I think this created a permanent rift in his relations with his father.

But to my father-in-law's credit, he did freely introduce his children to the many politicians then in Delhi, with whom he had been associated in his freedom struggle days. So the Subramanian homes, first in a government bungalow on Ranjit Singh Road and then on Rajendra Prasad Road and later on another Government bungalow on Pandit Pant Marg (which was then called Queen Mary's Avenue) hosted South Indian politicians like Rajaji and Kumaraswamy Kamaraj and Anantsayanam Aiyangar and Satyamoorthy Iyer; and Swamy was free to interact with them and did so. It was a broadening experience, which I cannot help contrasting with my own experience at roughly the same time in Delhi: like Swamy, we too were the children of a Government bureaucrat, brought up in Delhi in a Lutyen's bungalow on Tughlak Road; but though this was the exciting dawn of our first days as a free India, I cannot recall having interacted with anyone with political ideas. Actually our home was next door to Birla House which Mahatma Gandhi used to live in at that time; and I can recall occasionally accompanying visiting family friends from Bombay and Poona who would naturally come to listen at Gandhiji's prayer meetings.... We children would take our friends through the Tughlak Road servants' quarters which communicated at the back with the Birla House servants' quarters rather than through the more conventional front entrances. But I must confess with shame, this very privileged introduction left no impression on us as children. So much so that when Gandhiji was assassinated almost next door (my parents were then away on a trip to Almora), all I can recall is the servants locking the gates of our house to keep the milling crowds from bursting into our garden, while we stood on the gate planks and looked out at the grieving multitudes with no idea at all of the momentous event that was happening in front of our eyes.

IV

Anyway, Swamy grew up in the Delhi of the 1940's and 1950's, even personally experiencing the Partition era mayhem near his Ranjit Singh Road home. Swamy remembers that at one time his father was away in Washington at the height of the Delhi holocausts, without any way of contacting his Delhi family; and so an eight year old Swamy was expected to help by doing the marketing for the family. That was his first tentative connection with RSS volunteers which then were doing yeoman service in caring for beleaguered residents as well as refugees from Pakistan. On one occasion, in search of his uncle's dog, Swamy actually went alone through the horrible carnage of Turkman Gate, and when found, he was tied up for a day to the dining table leg as a punishment.

Swamy's parents had no Hindutva predilictions that I can discover; but the children also had another mentor, Kamal Singh. Kamal Singh was a teenaged Garhwali boy who had been sent to Delhi to search for a job. My father-in-law found him sobbing outside his home, took him in and gave him a job as a domestic. Later with enhanced qualifications and my father-in-law's guidance, Kamal Singh got a government job; but he continued to live with the family. It was he, who along with grisly man-eating tiger stories from his native Garhwali village, introduced Swamy to the Ramayana taking him along to the Ram Leela every year. (Years later when our girls were growing up, Kamal Singh performed the same educational introductions for them: our neighbour Mrinal Pande recalls daily seeing the three of them sitting waiting for the children's school bus while Kamal Singh told them stories or read from the Hindi newspapers for them).

Swamy's father allowed him to choose his own school; and he chose the DPS (the Delhi Public School) on Mathura Road (it was then called Church High School) partly because he liked the look of their school buses and partly because he liked the feel of going to school in a tent. For years the DPS functioned from World War II army issue tents while their school buildings were going up: it took a long time because apparently as fast as people contributed to the DPS building fund, the school's pioneer principal, an Anglican clergyman, spent the money on his own rather dubious concerns. Matters came to a head only because Swamy's next door neighbour, a Member of Parliament, Shri Shyamnandan Sahai, began to ask Swamy questions about his donations to the school fund; Swamy took the questions to the Principal; the Principal took Swamy out, and pointed out to him the building of the neighbouring Oberoi Hotel, which was then just coming up and said, "There, my boy, are your DPS School's buildings coming up"; Swamy naively so informed the Member of Parliament; an Enquiry came up and the Principal was defrocked and sacked: he seems to have been an enterprising educational genius because he went on to develop successive schools in Delhi; and with his swindling propensities, he was inevitably sacked from each of them in turn. He cannot have been an example of rectitude but I am told by Swamy that he was a splendid teacher and administrator, with a heavy hand on his cane, which Swamy felt occasionally.

Anyway, Swamy got a school education; though it cannot have been helped on by the fact that he would occasionally escape into the wilds of the neighbouring Purana Quila and the Delhi Zoo, then just coming up, and the newly developed Nizamuddin refugee colony which in a later, more fashionable avatar, became our home in the 21st century.

Swamy has never permitted himself to be put upon or patronised or ordered around. When the time came for him to apply for college admission, he went across to pick up an admission form from the very elite, very proper St. Stephen's College in Delhi. Apparently the snooty Anglican clerk handing out the forms took umbrage because Swamy was dressed in short pants; and told Swamy, "We don't give admission to babus." (in those days the word "babu" was used in the derogatory Kipling sense and did not, unlike today, connote a high ranking bureaucrat). Swamy did not attempt to argue with the clerk, walked across the road to the Hindu College and got admission there ….. It was St. Stephen's loss: Swamy loved his stay at Hindu College and is still fiercely loyal to Hindu, where as he puts it, the boys celebrated Diwali and visibly sneered at the Stephenians across the road who were reputed instead to celebrate Queen Elizabeth's birthday. Swamy played cricket and swam for the college and still got enough studying done to get a first in Mathematics…but of course that was not good enough for my father-in-law. Apparently he was continually holding up to Swamy as an example to emulate, a family friend, the toast of the Delhi Tamil Brahmin community, who had gotten the proper blue ribbon admission to St. Stephens and followed it up with the proper blue ribbon Oxbridge years……It turned out to be a disastrous toast. This gentleman, who I met years later and found friendly and inoffensive, had been given the good Tamil name of Ramaswamy Iyer; but, as was fashionable at St. Stephens, he took the improbable name of "Douglas" and liked to be called Duggie Ramaswamy. Well, Duggie became a physicist, (the approved job for a Delhi Tamil Brahmin), got married in the approved Tamil Brahmin fashion to another such Tamil Brahmin blue blood; and then proceeded to throw away all that kudos by divorcing his blue blooded wife and marrying an American. His name is naturally now mud in Tamil Brahmin circles. In the meanwhile after many ups and downs (mostly downs in their value system), Swamy, the one time black sheep, is looked upon with approval by Tamil Brahmins. I am not sure he returns the compliment.

V

As for Swamy, he proceeded from Hindu College to the Indian Statistical Institute (the ISI) in Calcutta. He learnt a lot there; but career wise it could not have been a wise choice. The Founder and Power at the ISI was Professor P.C. Mahalanobis, a crony of Jawaharlal Nehru who thought highly enough of him to make him Deputy Chairman of the Planning Commission, then a centre of awe inspiring power in the development of India on the Soviet model. Unfortunately Mahalanobis looked upon my father-in-law as a rival statistician, (my father-in-law founded the Central Statistical Organisation and had often crossed swords with Mahalanobis on issues purely of statistical knowledge), who had also earned his bale by refusing the Mahalanobis' offer to adopt his younger son. So when Swamy joined the ISI, he found a rather hostile environment: apparently even the teachers had been primed to give Swamy low grades. Things got so bad that Swamy was actually served notice of his possible expulsion. He recalls with gratitude the two professors who saved him: the Director Professor C.R. Rao who secured him a grace period of two months in which to improve; and Professor R.R. Bahadur who offered to take him under his wing and monitor him for those two months. It also helped that his father's (and indeed coincidentally my own father's) friend Dr. Tarlok Singh of the Planning Commission, introduced Swamy to a visiting Harvard faculty member Edward Mason.

The one other friend Swamy made in the ISI faculty was an unusual oddity, the anthropologist J.B.S. Haldane. Haldane hailed from blue ribbon Oxbridge, origins and Mahalanobis thought he had a feather in his cap when he secured him for the ISI faculty; but they did not hit it off. Haldane seems to have enjoyed revealing Mahalanobis' feet of clay; and he compounded it by refusing to give Mahalanobis his dinosaur bone: apparently Haldane had returned from an anthropological expedition in Central India, with a dinosaur bone; Mahalanobis had a special glass case made for the bone; but Haldane refused to hand it over insisting on keeping it collecting dust on top of his personal office cupboard. He seems to have hit it off with Swamy, and actually allowed him to finger the bone. Under his encouragement Swamy wrote his first paper, "Note on Fractile Graphical Analysis", a critique, disproving Mahalanobis' claims of originality for his own statistical invention, the pie-shaped sample which Swamy proved mathematically, was nothing but the first derivative of the Lorenz Curve.

Swamy, who has never lacked confidence in his ability, proceeded to send the paper for publication not just anywhere, but to Econometrica one of the most renowned Economics journals; and Econometrica not only accepted it but challenged the ISI intelligentsia to comment on it. Worse was to follow for Mahalanobis: Swamy, who (he insists it was under Mahalanobis' egging) had been given consistently low grades in all his courses at the ISI, applied for postgraduate admission to Harvard University and was not only accepted but granted a full scholarship. Mahalanobis got the ISI to write to Harvard enquiring whether Swamy had been given admission in the expectation that he would get an M.Stat. degree from the ISI, because, ISI said, it was not at all certain that Swamy would actually be awarded the M.Stat.. Harvard wrote back saying that there was no such expectation: Swamy had been given admission and a scholarship on the basis of the merit of his, "Note on Fractile Graphical Analysis" in Econometrica and his undergraduate results of a very high ranking first division.

So nothing more was heard of the proposed expulsion. Professor Bahadur sent in a report that if after this Harvard admission and scholarship, Swamy was expelled, "we will be the laughing stock of the whole academic community". Mahalanobis threw in the towel: as Swamy put it, perhaps with a little exaggeration, his ISI grades which had been consistently 0,0,0 suddenly became consistently A,A,A. In 1962 Swamy got his M. Stat. degree from the ISI and flew off to the U.S.. (As a footnote, I may mention that some years later when Swamy was on the Harvard faculty I was introduced to Mahalanobis who was visiting there: he insisted on taking all the credit for Swamy's discovery and subsequent success!)

Chapter III

FIRST DAYS IN THE US

I

At Harvard, Swamy lived upto his promise. In his first course, (he cross registered with MIT which was permitted by Harvard), given by the world renowned Professor Paul Samuelson, he pointed out an error in Samuelson's calculations on the blackboard, and won Samuelson as a friend for life. He got the right to work on his Ph.D. thesis within the breathtaking period of eighteen months (normally students budget on four years for this), and was accepted as his Ph.D. student by Professor Simon Kusnets, universally acknowledged as the Father of Econometrics. To help him finance his studies Kusnets got him appointed to the UN Secretariat as an Assistant Economics Officer. So Swamy moved to the UN in New York. But not for long. He simply did not find life as a UN officer (a job many Indians of that generation would have died for) sufficiently challenging, resigned his job and returned to Cambridge to work on his thesis.

It was a summer of penury: Kusnets was away for the summer and there was no stipend coming in, so Swamy starved through the summer on his meagre savings. It was a way of life, I later learnt to be familiarised with- though as a proper middleclass Parsi I never quite reconciled to it. For Swamy his mission always took first place; the means of survival was of secondary importance. And so dynamic has been his contrivance that somehow or other he has always managed to keep his head (and mine) above water.

II

In 1964, Swamy earned his Ph.D. two years after he entered Harvard which was a record, and joined the Harvard faculty. He was also made resident tutor at one of the exclusive Harvard undergraduate houses, Lowell House, where at mealtimes, he mingled with bright young undergrads, who discussed any and everything; and got Swamy educated on /addicted to American concerns and TV cartoons.

Surprisingly, one of his favourite breakfast companions was the resident English poet (later laureate): apparently he was happy to have discussions with someone like Swamy who neither knew or had pretensions to know anything about English literature. At formal Lowell House dinners too Swamy was much sought after to be seated next to: not for his scintillating conversation; but simply because Swamy neither smoked nor drank; so whoever sat next to him, got his brandy glass and cigar.

That year I came to Harvard and met Swamy. I married him two years later in 1966. My liberal father-in-law was quite approving; not so my orthodox Parsi grandfather. It was not that he knew any harm of "Madrasis"; and he certainly respected their brains, honesty, dedicated scholarship and unconcern over worldly success; but Grandpapa genuinely believed that Parsis were a race apart. As to "Madrasi" mores, he once told us a story of his bewildering experience while organising the annual session of the Indian Mathematical Congress in Poona. He had invited as guest of honour a learned Tamil Brahmin, for whom he was quite prepared to arrange simple obvious things like vegetarian meals; but he was flummoxed by the gentleman's other requirements: the learned gentleman asked for a room next to a well and a banana tree! Swamy when told the story was equally unsympathetic to his fellow "Madrasi's" requirements and dismissed him as typically "frozen in time": Swamy has no use for the non-utilitarian. But Parsis generally frowned on mixed marriages and my grandfather was the most stout opponent of this in the Poona Parsi community; and it took years for him to be reconciled to us though (he was a very honest intellectual) eventually he was forced to accept the truth of Swamy's statistical argument that the original Parsi shipload to India, reputed to consist of 96 men and four women could not possibly have produced the present Parsi community, (at one time the Parsi population rose to about a lakh), and there must have been intermarriage with local Indians. Swamy's later friend Prime Minister Morarjibhai Desai who hails from that area in South Gujarat, used to tell Swamy —possibly with some caste snobbery—that the intermixture was not with upper caste Gujaratis but with the local tribal Bhils; and he may have been right. Anyway, wherever we Parsis originated, Swamy and I went ahead and got married.

Like almost anything connected with Swamy, our wedding ceremony was somewhat unusual. Since our parents were not going to be present (though eventually we did manage to rustle up Swamy's mother, his sister Vatsala and her husband Srikantan (one of my most favourite persons), then a doctoral student in Michigan, and his American uncle Purshottam a medical Professor at Berkeley) it made sense to have it in Cambridge, in the U.S. where we were both based. My mother had only one request: it should not be a Hindu ceremony. A Hindu marriage can take place only between two Hindus; so when one of the parties is not a Hindu, Hindu pundits have devised a "shudhikaran" ceremony which "converts" the non-Hindu partner, whereafter a Hindu marriage ceremony can be performed. Thus my mother was advised, by such a conversion, I would lose my standing and rights as a Parsi.

I myself am no believer in Parsi ritual; but I was born and brought up as a Zoroastrian; I was initiated as one in our navjote ceremony; and I have a profound and abiding pride and belief in the ethics of Zoroastrianism, epitomised to me by a deep emphasis on truth, charity and trust worthiness and a simple Parsi creed "Good thoughts, good words, good deeds". I have never ceased to marvel that in the world of more than three thousand years ago, Zarthost Sahib had worked out such a perfect ethic, which continues to be practiced by us; I have no intention of renouncing such a wonderful heritage; and although my children have personally chosen to be Hindu, I know they are imbued with the outlook and ethics of my faith.

So our marriage was to be an American civil marriage, officiated at by a U.S. Justice of the Peace. Our friend, my co-religionist Rusty Kothawala, who was Head Tutor at Lowell House, recommended what he felt was a particularly sympathetic Justice of the Peace, a little out of the ordinary "Las Vegas" quicky-marriage style functionary. This was Dr. Te Yi Tsieh, formerly Ambassador of the Chiang Kai Shek Government to the U.S.. After the Chiang Kai Shek Government fled from Mainland China, Dr. Tsieh settled in Massachusetts, became a U.S. citizen and was appointed as a Justice of the Peace. At our request he offered to give us a civil marriage ceremony at our own home and we gratefully accepted. However, to our amazement, Dr. Tsieh did nothing by halves. He brought along all the paraphernalia of an orthodox Chinese wedding, including his gown, some of his prized statuettes of Chinese Gods, a Gong, incense sticks, silk scarves etc.; he lined them up, prayed to them and made us perform the correct Chinese responses; and so Swamy and I were married by him in a half hour Chinese ceremony. It was so elaborate and unexpected that half way through, I was at pains to keep from giggling. Years later when I described it to my senior Soli Sorabjee, Soli opined that it could not have been a totally legal ceremony since neither of us were Chinese or understood our responses. But I have a U.S. Government Certificate and Registration to prove otherwise.

It has also been a matter of pride for me, that ours was the cheapest marriage I have ever witnessed. Including the cost of the U.S. marriage license and Dr. Tsieh's ceremony, it only cost Swamy $40. My Indian and Pakistani friends (we all lived in the same Radcliffe Graduate Center dormitory) stood a cake, icecream, chips and cold drinks party to our guests; and perhaps the greatest expense was the exquisite Tanchoi wedding saris that my mother and aunts gifted to me, and the raw silk bandh gala that Mummy sent Swamy. The bandh gala arrived too late for the actual wedding so Swamy wore a brand new American suit and tie. And that was that!! He did not want to give me a ring because he said there was no provision for that in Indian ritual; but I felt it would be an indubitable proof of legitimacy so he got me a Sears Roebuck catalogue ring.

So nowadays, when people like our servants come to us for loans to carry out elaborate weddings for their children, I have on principle always refused them, pointing out that my marriage ceremony cost us only $40. Of course, that has never gone down well with them: they merely mutter that people of your status can get away with skin flint behaviour like that, but we have our family's "izzat" and expectations to consider.

At that time, even my conservative Parsi family, little though they relished a non-Parsi son-in-law, must have thought I was onto a good thing: Swamy was the youngest faculty member of the world famous Economics Department at Harvard University and the blue-eyed boy of at least two persons who later became Nobel laureates; and he was earning what Swamy has always mockingly referred to as a "Motu Motu Salary" (Gujarati for a large salary). The Delhi School of Economics was clamouring to have him join; and we decided to spend the summer of 1968 there.

III

Actually his thesis field of expertise was econometrics and index numbers. But Swamy has never been one to buck a new interest (in later years, out of sheer intellectual curiosity he researched deep in Indian history, then law and now Hinduism). India's disastrous China War took place while he was a student at Harvard; and it left him determined to somehow contribute his mite to his country. When John Fairbanks, Professor in the Department of Chinese Studies at Harvard offered him a slot in China studies (to be held concurrently with his assistant professorship in Economics), Swamy jumped at it. Typically he spent his first year there in studying not Chinese economics but the Chinese language Mandarin, acquiring in the process an unimpeachable upper class Mandarin accent and idiom. His next step was to collect all the radio broadcasts of the Communist Chinese Government and set me to work enumerating any data which referred anywhere to the price of anything in China. Only after that did he produce his first paper thereon, a comparative study of the economies of India and China.

The work was not received with approval by China scholars. In the 1960's and 1970's, American China scholars (and indeed almost all international China scholars and certainly the Indian Communist ones) were applauding the progress of the Chinese economy and comparing it very favourably with the progress of the Indian economy (which it was then fashionable to run down). Swamy used figures to show that in fact the Chinese figures for production were grossly exaggerated: I remember one point he made was that the Chinese economists inflated their production figures by using the figures for unhusked grain (unlike India, which truthfully reported only husked grain) and adding potatoes to their figures for grain production. (Later when we actually visited China and happened to interact with a visiting group of Indian population experts, Swamy discovered that in the Chinese countryside whole families were suppressing information by declaring only the first of their numerous progeny, which naturally skewed everything). So at the time, Swamy's figures were not generally accepted.

But some two decades later, Swamy got his reward: by then the Chinese were looking for cheap loans from the World Bank, only to be told that because of their superb economic performance they were not eligible. It was the Chinese economists who resurrected Swamy's figures to prove that China was not really as developed as Western scholars had claimed; and they got their cheap loans, and were correspondingly grateful to Swamy for having enabled that. One way or another, despite his capitalist and right wing thinking, Swamy has always had a deep and warm relationship of mutual respect with the powers in China; and he still is invited there almost every year. It has been one of Swamy's most heart warming experiences that unlike his experience with the time serving Indian intelligentsia, the Chinese have, rain or shine, loyally remembered him as a friend.

By the way, Swamy's professionalism requires him to insist on espousing the truth in statistical figures, even when it can prove embarrassing for his friends: just this year the

Union Finance Ministry (headed by one of his least favourite Party colleagues), announced that under the present Government, "the economy grew at 7.9.% in the fourth quarter of the last financial year and at 7.6% for the entire 2015-16 financial year". Such fancy claims cannot befool a trained economist and that too in his own special statistical niche as an econometrist; so Swamy diplomatically tweeted: "If I apply Samuelson-Swamy Theory of Index Numbers to India's GDP calculation or RBI interest rates, media will scream antiparty activity". A lot of bewildered politicians and journalists are still trying to figure out just what that means.

IV

Chinese and Chinese economics were not the only foray Swamy made outside the confines of his mathematical economic expertise. At one time, he got interested in the question of India's possible further nuclearisation, then a new topic. He studied the situation so thoroughly and then developed his findings in such a researched, fact filled paper that on its strength, his colleague Tom Schelling got him elected to the very exclusive Institute of Strategic Studies in London. After that, the then Head of BARC, Homi Sethna, invited him to visit BARC on his next trip to Bombay and there the exceedingly enthusiastic scientists (languishing in the neglect that followed the tragic fatal air crash of Homi Bhabha) took us all around their nuclear facilities and made Swamy conversant and up-to-date with the situation in the nuclear field in India. These were all the names which later after the Pokharan nuclear explosion, came to be known all over India; and their cordial initiation of Swamy into the up-to-date Indian nuclear world meant that for years after that Tamil papers used to refer to Swamy as "Bomb Swamy".

V

Actually, Swamy has the sort of enquiring researching mind that is attracted to all sorts of ideas; and when he gets interested, he gets down to the very bottom of it all, and proceeds to build thereon brick by brick. As a boy in school, he had never bothered to study his history textbooks, so his mind was uncluttered with any preconceptions on ancient Indian history. Things which to serious schoolgirls like me, were a given, such as the Aryan-Dravidian thesis, Max Muller's rather suspect dating of the Vedas and "the coming of the Aryans" and even the dating of more recent events such as the birth of the Buddha and the contemporaneousness of Alexander the Great and the Mauryas, were quite unknown to him. So when his friend and student Satish Singh introduced him to these ideas he got interested enough to spend several days in the research stacks of Harvard's Widener Library; and then he wrote a couple of learned footnoted papers, which he got vetted by Professor Zeph Stewart who taught classical history at Harvard. It is another thing that when he tried popularising his theses in India, the Indian History Establishment (a stronghold of the liberal left) refused to debate his ideas because they said haughtily Swamy did not have any formal education in history. I notice that these same experts are presently using the same tactics to discredit and blackball what they call the RSS school of history. But by now, hard irrefutable scientific research for example on the Harappan civilisation and the discovery of the Sarasvati basin, has progressed so far that the ideas Swamy had latched onto, are more or less established.

Again, in the 1970s, when back in India, I can remember Swamy and I were watching a TV programme on Singapore. Swamy noticed that all the street signs were in three languages: English, Chinese and Tamil; and suddenly it hit him to his shame that while he could read the English and Chinese signs he could not read those in his own mother tongue, Tamil. All my father-in-law's children were conversant with Tamil of the classic Brahmin variety (my father-in-law was founder of the Delhi Tamil Sangam); but they had been put in English language schools so they were not literate in Tamil. Swamy asked around in the All India Radio Tamil section which was then a stronghold of the Dravidian movement and where Tamil to match was spoken. So, thorough as ever, Swamy sat down to study not just the Tamil script but actually to study DMK Tamil, a quite more robust language than the polished cadences of his home and family. Then having studied the vibrant even bloodcurdling language that the Dravidian parties and the Tamil film world have raised to a proud fine art, Swamy decided this was not natural for him. Now he makes speeches in Tamil in Tamil Nadu, but the language he uses is the Sanskritised Tamil he was brought up on. When in my ignorance I have protested, "But Swamy, can the common Tamil really understand you!", Swamy has insisted that womenfolk, always more religiously conservative and devout and familiar with the Hindu scriptures, did indeed understand him. Besides, practical as ever, he has decided that a Sanskritised Tamil can be more easily followed elsewhere in India and so would do much to reconcile the anti-Hindi lobby in Tamil Nadu. Certainly, perhaps partially under pressure of the need for all India communication and jobs and mobility, the once fierce hostility to Hindi in Tamil Nadu, has fortunately become a thing of the past: so perhaps Swamy's decision has proved itself wiser in the long run. Certainly, too, his thesis appears to have been confirmed by the enormous success in Tamil Nadu, of Ramanand Sagar's teleserial, "Ramayan", which has turned out to be a great unifier of India.

VI

It was around this latter time that Swamy began to take a new look at his sartorial appearance. As a school boy and college kid in India he naturally wore the shirt and pant which by then was ubiquitous to his generation in our cities. His father, a Gandhian, almost always wore khadi; so as a Government bureaucrat he wore khadi pants and shirt to work, with possibly a jacket over that in winter. He belonged to a generation that was more comfortable in the south Indian dhoti, the veshti; so at home he would slip into veshti-kurta or even just veshti-banyan; but he never attempted to impose his preferences on his sons; and I think, except at his sister's wedding, Swamy had never worn dhoti-kurta.

In the U.S., Swamy therefore slipped naturally into shirts and pants with a western suit and tie for formal occasions.

In fact, he wore a suit for our wedding; and the only Indian style costume he had was a bandh gala coat, which my mother, not very familiar with "Madrasi" apparel, had got made for him as a wedding present. Of course, that was invariably teamed up with pants.

That changed a little on our first trip back to India in 1968. My uncle, who ran the Bombay turf club (where at that time, entry in dhoti-kurta was strictly barred), told us a hilarious tale of how he had had to procure a pant for a Marwari millionaire who had innoncently turned up to view a horse race, dressed in a dhoti. For the first time, Swamy saw the matter as an attack on the dignity of many Indians who were really much more comfortable in their traditional garments. So he went out and bought a couple of dhotis to wear on formal occasions to the discomfiture of my westernised family.

But of course in the U.S. there was no change in Swamy's attire, perhaps in part because regular and frequent laundering of a "six yard bed sheet" (that is what they were billed as by the local laundries) was expensive and problematic; and it could not be comfortably worn in the snows of a Massachusetts winter. It was only in India, after Swamy's first small steps into politics, when he began to make the Jan Sangh political travel circuit, that Swamy took to wearing dhotis regularly. Since his tutor in this was Atal Bihari Vajpayee, Swamy learnt to tie his dhoti in what is called the "kanyakubja" style: as a result very often dhoti cognoscenti after one look at him, took it for granted that Swamy must be from Kanauj. As to the numerous expensive American suits in his wardrobe, we handed them over to

Amit Mitra to distribute among the Bangladeshi refugees who were flooding India that year.

Then in the 1990s, Swamy changed base to Tamil Nadu; and adopted the South Indian veshti. But the veshti is simply a single yard long leg-length sheet which is tucked in place at the waist (for more vigorous activities like farming, you kilt it up to above the knee and keep your legs bare); so Swamy found it was often not possible to manage it with dignity especially if he had simultaneously to keep a hand free to carry two suitcases onto an airplane. At that point, he remembered that his late friend Rajiv Gandhi had Indianised his wardrobe simply by adopting pajama- kurta-waist-coat; so that's what Swamy did.

This year, all his experience in the garment line came to a head with angry comments, which are really quite undeserved. In June 2016, Swamy's tweet went broadcast, "BJP should direct our Ministers to wear traditional and modernised Indian clothes while abroad. In coat and tie, they look like waiters." The remark was not original: more than a half century earlier my maternal grandfather, a High Priest of the Parsis, who himself invariably wore the flowing white robes of his office, had introduced his son to Morarjibhai Desai, then Chief Minister of Bombay State. My unfortunate uncle happened to be dressed in coat and tie; and the ascerbic Morarjibhai took a dig at him by asking my grandfather in Gujerati, "And this, I suppose, is your butler?". That remark resonated with Swamy in the present century, when he noticed the then Finance Minister, (a Tamilian) who usually looked quite elegant in veshti and cuffed shirt, visiting Washington in a suit and tie. But the storm came about a decade thereafter when yet another Finance Minister happened to be visiting Beijing dressed in a suit and tie. The Press, primed to believe that Dr. Swamy was spoiling for a fight with the unfortunate Finance Minister, broadcast the tweet as a "personal attack" on him by an obnoxious Swamy; then the Congress Party's son-in-law got into the act with a spirited defence of the human rights of the humble Indian waiter; the usual headlines followed; and what Swamy had innocently intended as an off the cuff joke, became almost a cause celebre.

Chapter IV

RETURN TO INDIA

I

Swamy's return to India was typical. Our daughter Gitanjali was born in Boston, on New Years' day 1969. By that time, Swamy was definitely in line for tenure at Harvard. But, though he loved and respected the U.S. and all the red blooded Americans he bonded with so readily, (even now, when he studies or writes, he likes to have in the background TV news noises, not any of the Indian channels but the crisp CNN discourse made familiar by his student years in the US) he was very clear where his prime loyalties lay: his children, like he, were going to be Indians with Indian values in India. So when Gitanjali was a month old, he applied for an Indian passport for her from the Indian consulate in New York. Having got it, he relaxed being convinced that his daughter's future as an Indian was assured.

Swamy himself has always insisted on safeguarding his Indian nationality. When he joined Harvard as a faculty member, US law required that he change to a different visa and thereafter he could continue in the US usually on a "green card" (which is readily given to people with skills the US requires). But a Green Card requires that you swear to the intention of acquiring US citizenship and serving when required in the US Army–two things which Swamy felt would compromise his commitment to India. He refused to apply for a Green Card and prepared to return to India if necessary. Fortunately Harvard felt his contributions in two special fields, Mathematical Economics and China, were of such a calibre that the University itself wrote to the US Government that Swamy was needed for his rare expertise; and on this basis Swamy got repeated rarely granted Exchange Visitor Visa extensions that enabled him to stay without applying for a Green Card.

In any case, Swamy also decided that since children brought up for even a short while in the U.S., and going through the super patriotic nationalist U.S. school system, were ever after confirmed devotees of the Stars and Stripes and would not adjust to any other country, (a view reinforced fifty years later in the case of our grand daughter Tara who despite her name and blood lines, is an American through and through who as a small mite could proudly rattle off her "pledge of allegiance to the flag of the United States and the Constitution for which it stands") it was now time to work out a return to India.

Some twenty years later, Swamy discovered how wrong he was where Gitanjali's citizenship and Gitanjali's future was concerned. He had gone on a casual visit to meet the U.S. Ambassador to India for something else; there, equally casually the Ambassador told him that the U.S. had noticed that on several occasions, Gitanjali had entered the U.S. on an Indian passport, a practice, he said, which must cease.

"But, how else would she go? She is an Indian citizen." protested Swamy.

"She was born in the U.S.; and for us, she is a U.S. citizen; and she must enter the U.S. on a U.S. passport", replied the Ambassador.

We made further enquiries, as advised, with the U.S. consular section, who confirmed what the Ambassador had stated. Surprisingly, the U.S. had no objection to Gitanjali's also having an Indian passport: because they accepted dual citizens. It is India which does not recognise dual citizenship for Indians.

"Could she not give up the U.S. citizenship?", I asked.

The consul could not believe that anyone would even consider giving up something as precious as a U.S. citizenship. She put it into outraged words: "If she did that, we would see to it that she never stepped foot in the U.S. again."

So what were we to do? We put it to Gitanjali, then about to graduate from the I.I.T. Kanpur, with the offer of a postgraduate doctoral scholarship to the University of California at Berkeley. Gitanjali did not have any doubts: she accepted that she was a U.S. citizen, and applied for a U.S. passport. And she seems to have settled down there happily ever after.

II

Actually even before Gitanjali was born, Swamy had some earlier inducements to return to India. The Delhi School of Economics, impressed by his C.V, was anxious to have him on their faculty, and invited him to spend the summer of 1968 there.

Besides, every year, two or three of the Indian Heaven-born, the I.C.S.-I.A.S. clique, would land up at Harvard for a coveted one year study assignment, and of course, all of then took courses under Swamy. The 1967-1968 batch turned out to be one of the most exciting such groups. There was Kaushal Dass, of the last I.C.S. batch: a Lucknow product, who among other qualifications, had actually served in Madurai (which in his quaint Indian-Christian fashion, he pronounced as Madura) and also knew everyone and every institution in Delhi, and who like Daddy, knew every nuance of the Indian Government Rule Book and how to wield it. There was T.N. Seshan (by coincidence, Seshan too had once been Collector of Madurai), a totally orthodox Tamil Brahmin, with a background in, of all things, atomic physics, who was martinet enough to have terrorised all recalcitrant D.M.K. types in Tamil Nadu and was reputed to have ruled in the Tamil Nadu districts, with the sort of iron rod, that some quarter of a century later, he perfected as India's best known Chief Election Commissioner.

There were also two younger batchmates: the genial Jamsheed Kanga whose wife and I had been college mates, and there was Satish Singh, one of the most brilliant, dynamic and erudite minds I have ever met, who introduced us to an alternate history of India, the knowledge of which Swamy has since expanded and developed and fought to establish. Satish's ancestor, Kuer

Singh, a name to conjure with in Bihar, was one of the leaders of the rising of 1857, so contempt for the British version of Indian History ran deep in his blood, anyway; but he had built on that contempt with deep research into some of the new ideas on history which strangled by British education and the Indian establishment, were just emerging mostly in the vernacular. For example nowadays no reputable historian (except perhaps the die hard DMK ones) accepts the Max Muller inspired idea that a people called the "Aryans" had invaded India around the seventeenth or eighteenth millennium B.C. and displaced–"conquered"– the original inhabitants the Dravidians; but in our days it was routinely taught to us as gospel truth. Again on some rather specious logic we were taught that Alexander "the Great" had "conquered" parts of Northern India in the days of Chandragupta Maurya...another theory now well on its way out. But Satish had gone to original sources and to research available in Sanskrit and regional languages notably Telegu, to educate us in another view of history: Alexander was a contemporary not of Chandragupta Maurya but of Chandragupta Gupta, who ruled some six centuries after the Mauryas.....Indian history was being pushed back. It got Swamy, with an open mind and no previous knowledge at all of history to clutter it, not only to study it; but to actually write a couple of papers thereon. A decade later, in the late nineteen sixties and early nineteen seventies, there was a terrible outcry against him when he offered to publicly debate these ideas: the History Establishment simply ignored him on the usual plea (which they now use routinely to run down the "RSS school" of historians) that

Swamy had never done any recognised formal studies or courses in history...... But that was after our Harvard days.

I would reasonably have been expected to be the hostess of a scintillating group like this 1967-1968 ICS-IAS batch at Harvard; but my culinary skills are pretty low; and so my contributions ran to take-outs and pizzas. Fortunately both Kaushal and Seshan had brought their wives with them; and Usha Dass's and Jaya Seshan's cuisine was to die for (both were vegetarians though Usha was prepared to cook fish for her husband provided he cleaned it). So we not only had a year of brilliant and exciting discussions on India and its future but were extremely well fed in the process.

Actually there was a second concentric circle of friends we all shared who also cooperated to keep us well-fed and well informed about the situation prevailing in the Indian sub-continent: it was not only Indian civil servants who came to Harvard, but also Pakistani ones; and all of us discovered that we had more by way of a shared heritage, language and background in common with them than we had with other groups whether from the U.S. or other (what were called) "underdeveloped" countries. The group (with parts of which we are still in contact), was rounded off by my own particular friends –three Pakistani students with whom I had shared an apartment right through the 1965 Indo-Pakistan War (later in the 1970s one of them returned to West Pakistan, and two of them to Bangladesh) and a brilliant physicist from Hong Kong with whom Swamy could practice a common written language, Mandarin.

III

Finally earlier in that year Jaya Prakash Narayan (JP) and his wife Prabhavati had turned up for a few days at Harvard. There had been a terrible short supply of food production in India; the U.S. and particularly the Quaker welfare societies, had contributed hugely to prevent starvation deaths in Bihar; and JP was in the US to tour and thank these organisations. At that period, if any well known Indian turned up at Harvard, the University Marshall's Office generally got in touch with Swamy. Swamy was thrilled to meet JP: he had been brought up by a father who had been enthralled when JP, jailed during the freedom struggle, escaped from Hazaribagh Jail. We spent the next couple of days at JP's feet.

Swamy was a little flabberghasted when he first met him, to discover JP in a three piece American suit—whereas Swamy had taken pains to dress in his only bandh gala. But Prabhavati took in the situation at a glance; and berated JP, saying that it was disgraceful that a young expatriate like Swamy should know how to dress like an Indian on a formal occasion, which JP apparently did not! The very next time Swamy met them, JP was dressed in a bandh gala; and asked Swamy sheepishly, "Am I properly dressed now?".

JP felt that people like Swamy should return to contribute their skills to India's development. When Swamy confessed his interest in returning and told JP about the Delhi School offer, JP suggested that Swamy earmark a few months to be spent studying JP's Sarvodaya Movement and his followers. He offered to fit him in in the organisation he had built up in Madurai, near Swamy's "home town"; and Swamy enthusiastically accepted.

I should mention that when we did return to India in September 1969 and settled in to the Madurai establishment of the Sarvodaya, Swamy was not very impressed by it. Typically Sarvodaya volunteers were very decent, very dedicated and very selfless; but they also showed themselves quite helpless to deal with the evils and corruption so rampant in Indian society at all levels. Faced with an evil practice, their natural reaction was to lament, "Oh tempo! Oh mores!" And to retire from the field of battle. On the other hand Swamy has always taken on an evil practice head-on; and, if he thought it deserved to be acted on by him and destroyed, Swamy will work out a detailed strategy for its eradication and stop at nothing to carry it out, devoting immense time, patience and effort to this, unfazed by his numerous reversals. It is this philosophy that has made him so successful in attacking corruption. It has also made him quite a few enemies even among the numerous often quite decent people who will compromise with the corrupt, out of what they justify as "necessity" (a rather inapt translation of the Hindi word "majboori").

However the bond with JP continued for years. Whenever JP came to Delhi, we would visit him at his Gandhi Peace Foundation guest house; and Swamy and he would exchange ideas as to how they saw the future of India develop. There was a small period of coldness, when Swamy joined the Jan Sangh, because JP had the usual left wing inspired prejudices about "Hindu" nationalism; but that was only for a short period. When in the middle

1970's JP contacted Swamy again for ideas on how the Congress rot could be countered, Swamy told him bluntly that JP could not do it without returning to politics (JP like his Sarvodaya cohorts looked upon politics as a somewhat dirty thing). He introduced him to the Jan Sangh leaders JP had eschewed as untouchable (people like Nanaji Deshmukh who became his warm friend); and together they built up a People's Movement, that by 1973-1974 had set India on fire.

Chapter V

TWO JOBS AND TWO SACKINGS

I

Actually Swamy started out in India in 1968-1969 with the best of intentions. He really simply wanted to write his research papers and enlighten his extremely bright and focussed Delhi School of Economics and (later) IIT, Delhi students….. but alas that was not to be.

In 1968, in one summer semester of lectures (within the Delhi School of Economics and out on the wider "more desi" Delhi University ("DU") campus) Swamy lectured to what turned out to be extraordinarily enthusiastic "DU types". It even comprehended an article Swamy wrote that summer for—of all things—"Blitz", the pet paper of the left wing, reputedly read by "every station master in India". As is usual for all articles written by Swamy, it was a graphic, fact filled article where Swamy developed his then startlingly new thesis that with the infrastructure already developed, India could produce an atom bomb and delivery system for just a few lakhs – and it caught the attention of the Hindu right wing party, the Jan Sangh which invited Swamy to address their parliamentary party. To this audience, as he did (and still does) to anyone who would listen, Swamy talked on everything from the need for a Hindu Renaissance and the dating of history, to the need for a market economy, to India's ability to produce a nuclear weapon and delivery system.

Perhaps his speeches were too successful for his own good. They convinced an appalled Delhi University Establishment (correct secular communist-oriented career types) that Swamy (then teaching at Harvard) could lead a thought revolution that would sweep them and all their ideas off the face of the Campus. The fact that Delhi had just acquired its first Jan Sangh Administration must have been the final straw...hurriedly the Chair in Chinese Economics created at Delhi University, for Swamy, which Amartya Sen had promised Swamy "is being dusted and got ready for you", was put on the back burner. The Chair, by the way, remained unfilled for several years. Swamy was offered only a Readership, which was considerably less than what he already had at Harvard. So he refused. Finally sometime later the Chair was simply dismantled. I don't know what happened to the grants which had been used to establish it; but one can suspect they went to a deserving left wing cause.

And it was hoped no doubt that Swamy would stay put in the Wilds of America where people like him would not disturb the iron clad Soviet hegemony over the University of Delhi.

II

It did not turn out quite like that: Swamy, with his impeccable academic credentials, became Professor of

Economics at the I.I.T, Delhi; and settled in comfortably to tutoring the even brighter and more focussed kids who had succeeded in breaking into the toughest college entrance exam to enter the IIT portals. He had also been invited to join the faculty of the IIT Kanpur; but a short visit there and the discovery that the Delhi newspapers (replete with the political news he liked to start the day with) arrived at the IIT Kanpur only after mid-day, decided Swamy against Kanpur.

Again his decision did not work out quite so comfortably, this time for Swamy. In no time at all, the students, the Employees Union and the lower Faculty Staff were on Swamy's doorstep, pouring their grievances into Swamy's receptive ears. This did not make him popular with the IIT powers that be, since these included things like the degree of corruption that was involved in developing the Delhi IIT campus: the Director, (a construction engineer with no teaching or research qualifications that we could discover, but with an entrée to Indira Gandhi through his wife who was teaching Ikebana flower arrangements to the P.M. and her daughter-in-law Sonia), did not believe in building up a teaching program and was quite happy to let that be chosen by the IIT's British collaborators, while he himself spent the taxpayers money in constructing fancy buildings and auditoria over the whole campus, (the IIT had eight state of the art auditoria, quite unnecessary for such a small institute).

By now faced with an agitating Employees Union and students, the Director was determined to see that Swamy was not made permanent. His temporary appointment as

Professor was extended again and again. Finally a Selection Committee was set up. To make sure there was no unanimity and a consequent selection of Swamy, the Director set it up with nine members (an unusually large number); and since the requirement was that there must be a foreign expert on it, he asked around to find a suitably leftist foreign expert. Unfortunately for him since he did not know the field of economics well, he accepted the leftist recommendation of the foreign expert, Leon Hurwitz; and as Chairman of the Selection Committee he found someone from the reputedly left wing Delhi School of Economics. Once again, unfortunately for the Director, it was Professor Manmohan Singh, later Prime Minister of India, an unbiased scholar who looked only at the economics' contribution of the Applicant. When Professor Hurwitz realised that the Applicant was a co-author of a paper with Samuelson, he could only gasp, "That is something I would give my left arm for. Of course he must be selected!" (These were his exact words: I did not make them up). Professor Manmohan Singh concurred; and the rest of the Selection Committee fell in line. So Swamy was unanimously recommended to hold the Professorship; and got appointed; but he did not last as such.

Meanwhile to his investigation in corruption, Swamy had added a growing friendliness with the Jan Sangh. He even worked out for them an Economic Plan, entitled, "The Swadeshi Plan-An Alternative Approach to Socialism". Indira Gandhi poured scorn on it in a speech in Parliament where she referred to Swamy as a Santa Claus–people in vernacular India who were not really quite sure just what a Santa Claus was, suddenly heard of the existence of Subramanian Swamy. Thus between his agitation against corruption in IIT accounts and his Santa Claus Plan presented to the Jan Sangh, Swamy earned the ire of both the Director of the IIT and the all powerful Prime Minister of India. Within two years, Swamy was out on his ear, dismissed from the I.I.T with one months' salary in lieu of notice.

Chapter VI

AN ABORTED EVICTION AND OUR FIRST CONTEMPT OF COURT CASE AND THE AFTERMATH

I

But Swamy was not one to throw in the towel. He filed first a Writ Petition in the Delhi High Court; and when that got dismissed on a technicality (those were the days when employment in an "autonomous" Government institution was not held amenable to the Writ jurisdiction), he filed a humble Suit in the Tis Hazari District Court, praying for a declaration that he continued in the service of the IIT with all the perquisites attached thereto. A suit of that nature was guaranteed to mosey along for several decades (justice in India doth not travel on wings); but it came with one invaluable perk: Swamy got a Court Stay Order permitting him to continue to occupy the IIT flat he had been occupying when he was a Professor there.

But of course the IIT powers were having none of that. A sympathetic policeman warned us that the IIT had approached the local police station for a backup force as they proposed to evict Swamy by force from the premises.

Well warned, Swamy set off to his lawyers' place to collect the Tis Hazari Court's Stay Order; while the children, the cook and I settled down to wait for it. Unfortunately Swamy can never resist a political discussion; so on the way to the lawyers', he stopped off to have some discussion or other with his mentor Nanaji Deshmukh....

Meanwhile all hell broke loose on his peacefully slumbering family. Heaven knows how many trucks and beldars rolled up; someone got out and politely asked me to leave forthwith with my belongings as they had an IIT Eviction Order. I tried to explain that we had a Court Stay Order but Beldar types and the IIT official superintending the melee, do not know or respect such niceties; and as they moved threateningly to our threshold, I slammed the door in their faces, called in the cook as reinforcement, and we dragged all the drawing room and dining room furniture and piled it up against the beleaguered door which the beldars were hammering at. (We would have added the family beds to the barricade but those were upstairs and neither of us had the muscle power or time to add them to the mounting barricade). An hour and several fruitless calls to Swamy later (those were the days before the ubiquitous mobile made person to person communication a cynch), the police arrived and must have made the IIT minions see some reason, because they left; and the cook and I were left uncontested masters of the field.

I cannot remember what Gitanjali aged four and Suhasini (Chu) aged a couple of months were doing while all this hullaballoo was going on: with Swamy in the family I guess they eventually got used to fracas like that; but really that was our first brush with the LAW. And it was a victory !!!

After that there was no looking back as we continued our inevitable brush with the might of the Police and the Law.

II

Twenty years later, Swamy won his case against the IIT: his termination was quashed and he got a declaration that he continued all along in the service of the IIT with all salary and perquisites to date. But by that time Swamy was a Union Cabinet Minister and in no position to teach at the IIT, so he sent a letter resigning from the IIT and claiming his back wages till that date. The IIT accepted his resignation; but we are still battling for the back wages. By now, a further quarter century later the back wages with interest thereon, alone works out to nearly a crore; but IIT still soldiers on and so do we.

Some clever lawyer had found what he thought would shut off Swamy's claim to back wages. Under Fundamental Rule 54 and 54 (A) of the Government of India Service Rules, when a dismissed employee is declared reinstated, the Government is entitled to deduct from his back wages whatever such employee has earned elsewhere while under dismissal. So IIT wrote to Swamy demanding to know what he had earned at Harvard while out of his job, so that they could subtract this princely sum from the back wages due. In those days, wages at IIT were ridiculously low: somewhere in the Rs. 1000 to Rs. 2000 per month range for a full professor—I remember my colleague Harish Salve, who appeared for Swamy at one stage in the convoluted law suit, goggling at a figure which did not even match the clerkage he paid his clerks per appearance; and if from that was subtracted what Swamy had earned in an eighteen month stint at Harvard, (and that multiplied by the appropriate rate of exchange from dollar to rupee), no doubt we would have ended up with no back wages at all.

On the other hand we have pointed out that IIT is not the Government of India and so it is not covered at all by F.R. 54A-a stand surprisingly supported by the Union Education Ministry. The suit of course, like everything legal in India still goes on, so we have not yet come into this windfall.

III

Swamy has a theory that all Parsis react like tigers when it comes to an attack on their right to their private property; and he says it was manifested to him by my tigress reaction to the Beldar Attack on my home and goods. Certainly by now we were quite ready to sick the law in all its contempt-of-court-Majesty on the errant IIT authorities. We took the matter back to the Learned District Civil Judge's Court which had granted us a stay of dispossession from our home.

With the Police Station Report as our basic document (that the IIT had asked for police backup and had then proceeded to sick their beldars and bailiffs and buses on us), the Learned Judge had no alternative but to hold that prima facie the IIT had disobeyed a Court Order staying our dispossession; and that prima facie, the IIT was guilty of Contempt of Court. We sat back and waited smirking for the IIT to get its cum uppance.

But the IIT was nothing if not resourceful. Before the District Judge, they pleaded that they had no knowledge of the Stay Order. We objected because we had personally monitored its service on the IIT. The Judge sent for the Dispatch Record Book. It came complete with the signature of whoever had received the intimation of stay….. and… would you believe it ?,… a whole bottle of ink had been poured over the page and the signature was unreadable. The Judge was forced to call off the Contempt Notice as it was impossible to figure out as to on whom the Intimation of Stay had been served and hence which precise scofflaw should be named for contempt of court!

IV

Clearly it had been demonstrated that the Law in all its Majesty was for humble people like us, not for the State and its minions. But by then Swamy was hooked on his first law suit; and was happily to expand on that over the next half century….. he is by now a recognised AUTHORITY on all sorts of Law, without the benefit of a law degree (whether genuine or the bogus one that AAP politicians collect from the wilds of Bihar).

Interesting too was the Delhi elite reaction to Swamy's dismissal. By their eschewing of any contact with him (and in contrast to the way they had fawned on him when he was just visiting from their Mecca, Harvard), the Delhi elite (from the Lahore Punjab Provincial Service types right across the subcontinent to the Presidency College-Oxbridge

Bengalis) made it clear that they were happy Swamy had gotten his just deserts ….Swamy's mentor Kaushal Dass, himself by birth and training a member of this extremely successful class, used to refer to their attitude as "Le trahison des clercs", a phrase (meaning literally the treason of the clerks), made famous by Bendels 1927 book of that name, where the author castigated this attitude as the betrayal by the intelligentsia of their vocation as intellectuals. But then perhaps, our "clercs" had a racist streak as well as an occupational prejudice to them, and could not conceive that a Madrasi who probably ate with his fingers, was really entitled to consort with them in their rarified forks-and-knives eyrie in the IIC (the India International Centre) at Delhi. The Madrasi Brahmins could see the injustice dealt out to Swamy; but they were practical people, dependant on and wedded to their salaries, TA and DA; and they felt that Swamy had quite foolishly given these up for a mere principle. My unworldly father-in-law's reaction was typical: he told Swamy, "You should have got yourself confirmed as a permanent professor (Swamy had gotten himself sacked while he was still on some sort of extended probation) before you decided to fight the Establishment".

The suggestions that other "well wishers" gave, bordered on the ludicrous. Indira Gandhi's right hand man, Gopalaswami Parthasarathy, a family friend of the Subramanian clan, actually suggested that Swamy should change his name and try and get a job of sorts (he suggested "travelling salesman in Bombay") where his iniquities were not broadcast…. But of course that was all water off a duck's back.

Perhaps the "Bombay" suggestion was more significant, nay sinister than you can imagine in present day unashamedly capitalist India. India of the 1960s and early 1970s was securely in the grip of the Soviets. This was not just indigenous naïve left liberalism: a whole generation of upperclass Indian intellectuals had been reared (brainwashed) in the post war English universities where it was fashionable not just to be left but actually Communist (witness the Cambridge group assimilated under Kim Philby and Antony Burgess and the like, which mentored post war Indians of the Mahalanobis to Parthasarathy to even as late as the Amartya Sen school). For these persons' interests (ideological as well as personal), it was vital to ensure that the stranglehold on India of the Soviet model of socialism be ensured for all time; and in this respect the "Bombay" group had stood out as dissenters with an alternative approach; in any case, Bombay, unlike Delhi and Calcutta, has always been more concerned with commerce than with politics, and its thinking tends to be rightwing. So actually Parthasarathy's plain and blunt lecture to the Swamy of 1972-1973, could have had sinister connotations: Parthasarathy not only gloated about the Soviet hegemony over India and its stranglehold over all centres of power and patronage; but even implied that Swamy could expect no relief from his US friends and contacts, because Russia and the U.S. had already partitioned the world between them and had accepted that India would remain in the Soviet sphere.

Swamy who can quietly maintain a grudge for decades finally got back at Parthasarathy in the late 1980s. All through the Indira Gandhi years, Parthasarathy had been the accepted doyen of foreign policy; and so when Rajiv Gandhi became Prime Minister, he naturally hoped to continue as such. He presented himself to Rajiv. Unfortunately Swamy who happened to be just visiting Rajiv then, was sitting in the next room, and Rajiv, unsure in his knowledge of foreign policy had happened to turn to Swamy on this point; and it took Swamy no time at all to pour scorn on Parthasarathy's qualifications and achievements. Parthasarathy got no post under Rajiv.

But the likes of Parthasarathy apart, Swamy had elsewhere too a lot of "black listing" and "black-outing" to contend with off-and-on over the next decades. Again perhaps from the Soviet Union, the Delhi elite—governing classes, intellectuals, journalists-in-the–upper-echelons, media lions, the "clercs" as defined by Kaushal Dass—had developed the concept of the "non-person" and how to deal with this animal: you black him out of all possible press coverage (certainly all favourable coverage), and make sure he does not get invited to lectures, seminars, even elite parties: also if it became necessary to refer at all to him, it must be done from a plane of judgmental superiority and concentrate on Swamy's shortcomings, moral and intellectual and–most criminal of all—"communal". I found that it was considered quite acceptable in polite circles to refer to Swamy (who to my knowledge, has never lifted a physical finger against anyone) as "that young ruffian". The critics did not hesitate to be downright dishonest if necessary: one eminent editor spread far and wide his "information", that Swamy had never actually been to

Harvard at all: we learnt this from his junior who having lived with us during her student years in Boston, could hardly back up his lie.

With Swamy, this "non-person" treatment did not continue sustained and uninterrupted and at all times; for example when Swamy became an M.P. and later a Minister, he could at intervals be flooded with attention (not always welcome!) Also, for some reason the diplomatic world in Delhi did not appear to have any instructions in this regard because Swamy continued to be invited to a lot of embassy parties. Perhaps the diplomatic world had a professional interest in news collection about the real India at grass root level rather than the artificial Delhi of the ruling elite (I think I shall designate it as "Lutyens Delhi" because the ordinary middleclass and trader Delhi coverage of (even benign interest in) Swamy continued over all the blackout years). Also, the press blackout did not appear to extend beyond the English language "national" press and definitely it did not appear to be enforced/enforceable outside of Delhi. So very often, friends and contacts elsewhere than in Delhi would phone us up to tell us of some news item about Swamy that had been carried in their local press. Or they would post us a press cutting. Also, until in the 1990s the designation of Swamy as a "non-person" was extended to RSS and BJP strongholds, the reportage in the Sangh press and the invitations to Sangh seminars continued unaffected by Lutyens Delhi pressures. I maintain a press cuttings file from 1968 onwards; and a statistical study of this record could provide someone with a thesis grade study into the Swamy blackout.

I recall one example of how the blackout can work. When Swamy had just returned to India and was still persona grata, the broadcasting mandarins had thought it would be a good idea to give him a slot to speak on Chinese economic issues, to be beamed by All India Radio worldwide. Although apparently the Chinese authorities jammed it, it continued for a few months during which time an influential "Lutyens Delhi" professor V.P. Dutt in the Delhi University Chinese field, decided that Swamy was muscling in on his monopoly to broadcast on all things Chinese. Now V.P. Dutt had an excellent network in the Delhi bureaucracy, the "clercs". He lobbied with them; they said they needed some criticism of Swamy's broadcasts. V.P. Dutt approached his friend the well known journalist Amita Malik. Amita Malik neither knew economics nor did she understand the Chinese language; but she obliged Dutt by writing an article in which she castigated Swamy's column as "boring". Swamy lost the radio broadcast slot…..in his defence, as anyone who has read his articles and books would endorse, I can imagine all sorts of aspersions (valid or otherwise)cast on his writing,-….. communal, biased, right wing, slanted, downright evil,… but "boring"?

Perhaps I am straying very far from this early period (the 1970s), but this may be a good place to lay before you my thesis of what finally broke the back of the Lutyens Delhi blackout: I credit it to the internet age and the development in the twenty-first century, of the private TV channels (which were no longer appendages of the Government Doordarshan).

At that time, Swamy developed a "twitter" following. I cannot pretend to have very much knowledge of the way it functions; but Swamy studied it thoroughly, grasped what a marvellous way it was to keep in touch with a brave new open-minded world and he took to it like a duck to water. The result was that by the second decade of the twenty-first century, first hundreds and then thousands and then lakhs and finally a couple of million (it presently hovers over three million) enthusiastic, tech savvy and terribly open-minded men and women, young and old, began to look forward to opening their day by seeing what Swamy had to say on Twitter. They would reply in their lakhs; and Swamy would personally respond as and when he found something promising and thought provoking. Unlike most twitter followings of a mammoth size (I am told the record followings are those of the Prime Minister and Amitabh Bachan both of whom hire professionals for it) Swamy's twitters bear his own unmistakable stamp and are not conducted by some agency or website on behalf of Swamy.

I cannot help contrasting this with a feeble attempt I made in 1977 to reach out to Swamy's then following. The Emergency had got over; there was a Janata Government in place; and the floodgates were forced open by people who had had to suppress their aspirations and grievances over the Congress years. To them, Members of Parliament like Swamy brought new hope: he was deluged with mail (in those days people could communicate only through the postal service, the rather shaky telephone services and by hand). Touched by their genuine woes, I took on the task of cataloguing and replying; but it was impossible to make any sort of meaningful dent on the flood. The more I replied the more they wrote. After a time reminders began to pile up. I recall on our first train trip from Delhi to Swamy's Bombay Parliamentary constituency, I took along several tin trunk loads of correspondence in the hope that Party Workers in the Bombay North East constituency could pitch in; but it did not work out.....with communication what it was in the 1970s, it could not have.

Another phenomena that played its part in breaking the back of the Swamy blackout was the development of private television news channels in the present century. Till then there was only the Government (that is effectively Congress) monopoly on the terribly insipid and uninspiring Doordarshan. I can remember that when we returned to India in 1969 the highlight of the evening programme was something called Krishi Darshan which may have enlightened the aspiring farmer but drove normal bored viewers away from their television sets in droves. Also intellectuals with the proper political ("leftwing" and Congress) credentials were allowed unlimited access to All India Radio and Doordarshan; but naturally they too tended to bore the hell out of their audience. Otherwise almost the only good unbiased fare on offer were the vernacular film re-runs which were excellent but did not make people think deeply on matters political. Matters picked up when (I think it was in the late 1980s), there came the era of the gigantic serials the Ramayana and the Mahabharatha: it became evident that the vast millions of Indians were deeply attached to their Hindu heritage. But even that did not revolutionise the news coverage: that had to wait for when

TV was opened to private news channels and cable TV; and thinking people began to watch politically lively programmes.

The age of the evening Brains Trust (on the lines of what was already available on BBC and CNN except that our Indian Brains Trusts tend to be noisier, less Parliamentary and more dogmatic and untruthful) was established; but of course, the English main line channels (which subsist on elite advertisement of the limousine and luxury apartment and disguised liquor variety) continued to be monopolised by the "Delhi elite". They still are; but something has forced them to bend to necessity. Vernacular TV audiences (which is of course most of India, both rural and urban and whose advertisement revenues depend on humbler products like underwear and pickles) has no particular loyalty to or empathy with the views of the Lutyens elite. Swamy began to be invited thereon. Once these private channels discovered that Swamy had garnered a rather spectacular TRP (Television Rating Point Count), they could not have enough of him. The thin edge of the wedge was inserted; to enhance their TRP, the English main line private channels were forced to feature Swamy; and the blacklisting of Subramanian Swamy is, at least for the present, very much a thing of the past.

As I was completing the last paragraph, something happened to shatter my complacency; perhaps blacklisting was not such a bad thing: at least it was restful. But there is nothing restful about the barrage of Lutyens Delhi inspired news items about Swamy that hit the headlines in the month of June 2016.

Like a lot of Swamy's fracas, it started out as a scholarly dispute. Sometime in the 2013's, the UPA (i.e. Congress) Government, which had earlier appointed an Indian American scholar Dr. Raghuram Rajan, as Chief Economic Advisor, promoted him to the very influential post of Governor of the Reserve Bank. Swamy has professional reservations about "Governor" Rajan's (in contrast to his eight predecessors, Dr Rajan likes to be called "Governor Rajan"–an American title not commonly used in India) fiscal measures; and wrote against these even during Dr. Manmohan Singh's term as P.M. Nevertheless "Governor" Rajan, who had a three year term, continued in office even after the Modi Government was in place. Swamy persisted in his "Governor" Rajan criticisms; but matters only came to a head when Swamy started writing against "Governor" Rajan's getting a second term as Governor; and perhaps because of this criticism, perhaps because of a Government indication that it was quite content not to controvert Swamy's statement, "Governor" Rajan was forced to opt out of a possible second term.

Lutyens Delhi seeing its ewe lamb being taken away, fell en-masse on the villain Swamy (particularly since he had followed it up with assorted tweets about other possible targets in the economic bureaucracy); and nasty cooked up lurid stories about him and his due come-uppance became the headlines of the day. It might have been reasonable to have the opposition to Swamy and his views tucked away in the back pages of the Delhi Press; but that is not the Lutyens style: so Delhi was regaled with Swamy headlines and news broadcasts and Evening Brains Trust sessions—not all of them necessarily truthful.

In his unique fashion, Swamy hit back. He simply refused to take any calls at all from the Media until he got an apology at least for the broadcast lie (assiduously circulated by a snake-in-office and carried uncritically by all the Lutyens Media) that Swamy had been called in and hauled up by the P.M. for this crime. But the Media, seeing its TRPs slipping away, would not take no for an answer. Hordes of journalists and their dish ornamented vans blocked the road in front of our home; his mobiles rang and rang though Swamy determinedly refused to accept Press calls; and for two days whenever Swamy left the house, his security had to smuggle him out through the servant's entrance. From the perspective of the non-person's family, there is a lot to be said in favour of the anonymity inflicted on the "non person"; but unfortunately that is not Swamy's style.

Swamy's strategy has worked. Within two months, most of the media have made the demanded peace offering; and you can once more see Subramanian Swamy grinning in person on TV instead of merely the scrolled announcement "Subramanian Swamy says this or that".

Chapter VII

SOME VINDICATIONS OF SWAMY'S PHILOSOPHY RE THE NON-NECCESSITY FOR CORRUPTION: SWAMY STUMBLES INTO THE REAL ESTATE WORLD AND THE AUTOMOBILE ACQUISITION WORLD

This Chapter develops some instances in Swamy's life, which vindicate his two fold philosophy/thesis:

(1) That the goods of this world are to be acquired only to improve one's efficiency and efficacy;
(2) When one really needs something, one merely holds out one's hand and the Heavens drop in the required article.

You may recall the promise I made in Chapter II: "Lest some cynical reader feels that the above analysis of Swamy's philosophy is unbelievable, in Chapter VII hereafter, I give a few significant instances of how this principle has worked in Swamy's life." Here is how this developed.

I

To get back to my interrupted narrative, anyway, in 1972-1973, between Delhi University, IIT, Indira Gandhi, the Delhi elite and the Left, it looked as if there was to be no place in India for a self respecting intellectual like Swamy. Fortunately the threats did not work. Swamy even got an unlooked for bonanza from the IIT's attempted eviction, viz. the foundation of his personal fortune. Since by then Swamy had become somewhat well-known, the newspapers covered the aborted eviction; and thus something which respectable people would prefer not to have become known, (so far, as far as we knew, forcible eviction happened only to Dickensian paupers) came to the knowledge of my super respectable family..... only my father did not react with the holy horror and disapproval I had expected. He came to Delhi to tell Swamy,

> "We are not the kind of people who go through things like this attempted eviction; and who knows, they may make yet another attempt. So I think you people should get another house and you should move into it."

Swamy protested that he certainly did not have the money to rent another place. And Daddy said he thought it would be better if we bought a house, and he was prepared to "help" us. He was as good as his word. In a very short time with the help of a very nice broker Balram Bhasin, recommended by Swamy's friend and fellow Jan Sanghi Vijay Malhotra, (then Chief Executive Councillor of Delhi, the then equivalent of Delhi's later Chief Minister) we went house hunting.

It was not all that easy. My difficult father with Bombay notions on realty, insisted that it had to be a freehold property; and in the early seventies in South Delhi only two colonies were freehold—Hauz Khas and Greater Kailash I –(most elite South Delhi-ites i.e. people with "approach") expect as a matter of right to get highly subsidised plots from the Government, which plots in those days were leasehold) and both these two freehold colonies were meant for fairly wealthy people; but we persisted and found what to us seemed the house of our dreams: 300 square yards, single storey, 3 bedrooms with attached baths, drawing dining and kitchen. A court yard in the middle where I could dream of making a garden patio, overlooked by the glazed sliding doors of the dining room and kitchen, a pocket handkerchief garden in the front with a lawn and six rose bushes, a driveway to park our sole valuable possession our "biscuit van" Mahindra four wheeler Jeep (purchased with almost all our US savings so we could carry out my dream of a Bharat Darshan of the picturesque countryside—it was only later that I discovered that my dream was not shared by Swamy who would much rather have bought an airplane so he could whizz from point to point, oblivious of any picturesque countryside in between), a yard at the back just large enough to house three small guava trees (perennially raided for their fruit, by the local children) and our only other possession, a large bouncy mongrel, Winny, of no value whatsoever who had earned the curses of the IIT campus with his depradations.

II

The house was priced to start with at the awe inspiring sum of Rs. 2 lakhs, which of course neither Swamy nor I possessed. So my father asked, "Well, how much can you afford?". Swamy gulped and said," Rs. Ten Thousand."

"Well", Daddy told the broker, "That will be the earnest money." (Within four years that Rs. 10,000/- turned out to be another bonanza for Swamy at my expense, as I shall show you in the course of my story).

Daddy then got down to the brass tacks of negotiating the price: and he was pretty shrewd about it, pointing out that the seller could not produce proof that the boundary wall was on "our" side of the property; and bringing down the final price to 1,45,000/- (which my father paid from my funds with him) over and above Swamy's earnest money of Rs. 10,000/- We were lucky. Apparently the seller (he turned out to be an uncle of the Congress Party's future son-in-law, Mr. Vadra) was in a great hurry. He had bought the house to persuade his English wife to move to Delhi and he had furnished it (down to the curtains); but the wife was not to be enticed, so he was selling it so that he could return to live (happily ever after we hope) in England. From our experience with him, he deserved to be very, very happy. Eventually, in return for Swamy's earnest money, the seller handed over to us all the house's furniture and the curtains.

We needed all that furniture and the curtains: there simply was not enough money left with us to curtain all those large glazed spaces that the house doors and windows ran to. Left to our own tastes we might not have run to sturdy full length white and silver striped drawing room curtains, white and pink striped children's room curtains and white and yellow and black striped spare room curtains. Also a rather revolting ochre coloured sofa set (mustard with a black thread running through, and a series of improbable padded arches as the backrest) in the front room. But we had to live with them. We even had to live with the fancy ochre coloured stuffed sofas, because our own humble furniture consisted only of beds and more beds elevated by the name of "diwans" (i.e. a legless bed with a mattress and bright coloured cheap cushions and bolsters). The worthy Mr. Vadra even threw in a formica top dining table and plastic covered chairs; and (joy of joys) a writing table, and many very occasional tables with smoky black glass. All these had curious legs attached at an elegant slant rather than the more usual vertical legs.

There were even built in formica wall cupboards (to hold our humble clothes), and built in formica sideboards (to hold our humble dishes) and built in formica display cases (no doubt to display our humble non existant bric-a–brac) again with slanted legs, and a real live built in kitchen to die for. The final touch of genius was a "chor khana" behind the built in dressing table. (We were thrilled with that chor khana... how could anyone even begin to guess it was there? ....we were very naïve: at the very first thorough strip search of our home by the Enforcement Directorate, its blood hounds zeroed in unerringly on that chor khana)...but I am running ahead of my narrative to the bad days of the Emergency when police depredations made that first attempted IIT eviction appear like a bean feast. But all that in its proper place.

Later we discovered that all the inspired built in cabinet work owed its origins not to the worthy Mr. Vadra, but to the old lady, Suhagvanti who had actually built the house (her dream home) for herself, before her family sold it to Mr. Vadra. It all went up in splinters when we finally sold our home to the builders who bulldozed down the house (which by then had run to two storeys to facilitate our burgeoning careers) to put up very high priced flats on the land. As for Mr. Vadra's furniture, I thankfully donated it to the Indian Women's Press Club, (of which my sister Coomi was a founder member) which had the good taste to pass it on a few years later. The curtains, by the way, were so sturdy that they still survived; but by then (Chu was getting married and I thought we needed a change of decor), we had become strong-minded and affluent enough to get more acceptable replacements.

III

If I may be permitted to run ahead of my narrative, I think this is a good place to set out all that House's contribution to Swamy's future wealth—all acquired quite painlessly.

Well as I related above, Swamy's contribution towards payment for the House was Rs. 10,000/- the earnest money; and Daddy's contribution was Rs. 1,45,000/- plus the stamp duty and taxes of Rs. 11,600/- (all from my bank account which Daddy administered); the Broker, by now a firm friend, seeing our penurious plight refused to charge us anything as brokerage. Finally as icing on the cake it turned out that the resourceful Mr. Vadra had managed to convince the Delhi Municipal Corporation that the ratable value of the property (i.e. the value of the property in municipal records) was an astounding Rs. 10,800/- on which we paid Rs.1,160 as annual property tax. I don't know who was the most in transports over this piece of information: the canny broker, my frugal father or us feckless persons who now saw our annual budget scarcely broken by our newly acquired property and property tax thereon.

But then Swamy has always been lucky: when and where money was needed, it had a habit of turning up. The further ramifications of our first major property deal went on multiplying.

In 1976, when he was on the "Most Wanted List", Swamy appeared in Parliament, made a short speech and disappeared with the result that a large section of the Police of the country was set to work to locate and nab him one way or another. The Police had no clue how to nab him; but they did know the Code of Criminal Procedure (which herein after I shall, as they say in all lawyers briefs, refer to "for brevity"as the CR.P.C.). Therein is laid down how you have to proceed against an absconder: you attach his property. This is not to be done lightly or at break neck speed. As I discovered by a thorough reading of the relevant sections of the then C.R.P.C., the Police is required to affix, "on a conspicuous portion" of his property demands for him to appear, to go into the marketplace and by drum beat call on him to surrender on pain of attachment of his property and only then should they carry out the painful procedure of taking it over.

Well the Police, during the Emergency, under pressure to instantly produce Dr. Swamy did not have the lengthy luxury of following the procedure including the drum beat in the marketplace. Within 24 hours they had served me with notice of attachment, and despite my indignant demand for the formality of the drum beat, (Heaven knows why I should have wanted the whole neighbourhood and its marketplace to learn of Swamy's disreputable outlaw status!) they had walked off with all Swamy's presumed portable property.

The list of goods attached was rather pathetic: 2 cars, a TV and an air-conditioner. In an attempt to save Swamy's books from the garnisheeing, my sister-in-law Sushila and I had spent the previous night writing my name on the flyleaf of all Swamy's books; but it was a wasted effort: the Police was simply not interested in accumulating a library on Economics and Statistics. They did not even want the hassle of taking over furniture, linen, cookware and such like. For them property meant consumer durables and real estate.

Naturally they had set their eyes on the HOUSE; but that required getting a declaration from a Court that it was not my property but Swamy's; and since it was clear that all cheques but the initial Rs.10,000 cheque were signed by me, it was not that easy to get it so declared. So for that they started the process of getting the Income Tax authorities to declare my name on the house as merely benami. It took all the duration of the Emergency and part of the following year to get that done; and meanwhile we were left in possession with a roof over our head.....but more of that anon.

My cook informed me that she was not prepared to work in a refrigerator-less kitchen, and the refrigerator was indubitably paid for by Swamy by cheque; but I had an airconditioner with a bill settled by my father's check; so I made a swap with the Police. They attached the air conditioner (I would not have been able to afford its electricity consumption anyway) and left my cook in possession of the fridge.

As to the ownership of the house, that was fought over by my Chartered Accountant with the Income Tax authorities. Sometime towards the end of the Emergency, the Income Tax authorities, flying in the face of the cheque payments, decreed that it had "always been Mrs. Swamy's intention to share the ownership of the house with Dr. Swamy"; and they directed that we each were owners of a half share of the House....so the way was clear for the Police to attach Swamy's half share.

We went in appeal. The Appeal, fortunately decided after the Emergency was over, mindlessly confirmed Swamy's ownership of a half share in the House. Swamy's only contribution was to get me a meeting with the then Finance Minister, my father's old friend Mr. H.M. Patel; and he slept through my entire exposition of my case before deciding that the Appeal Order appeared to be correct. I wanted to go to the I.T. Appellate Tribunal; but then my C.A. put his foot down. He pointed out that normal people went to enormous lengths to get an order like ours (so that the tax liability of each half owner was halved), so it would be truly feckless of us to fly in the face of such a godsend.....I gave up; and Swamy with his Rs.10,000/-

investment became half owner of the house; and when it was finally sold in the 1990s, his half share came to in the vicinity of half a crore…not at all bad for a mere Rs.10,000/–investment. Since this was at the expense of my share, I was the only loser;… and Swamy owed the windfall only to the IIT's attempts to evict him in the 1970s. He was not suitably grateful to the IIT.

We were not as fortunate when after the Emergency the Police handed back our attached possessions. The air-conditioner and the TV still worked; but, as I will explain a little further down, the jeep was a disaster;—about the only loss Swamy made in the whole attachment fracas.

IV

The next bonanza Swamy tumbled into was even more splendid. If you will permit me to digress a little, by about twenty years, to 1992 when we bought our house in Dehradun.

It all started a few years earlier when we spent a weekend with his aunt Amala, at her lovely hundred year old bungalow on the then outskirts of Dehradun, next to a Reserve Forest. We had a room overlooking the hills and my heart melted when Swamy after spending a peaceful morning writing, heaved a contented sigh and said it would be so nice if he had a place near the hills where he could escape and write to his heart's content. Of course such a huge and lovely house and garden (it was really an orchard with hundred year old mango trees, fifty year old litchi trees and thirty year old pumelo trees and a few guavas and loquats, to which I later added grape fruits and avocados) were beyond our wildest aspirations; but by then we had a little money saved up; and Amala mentioned that she was contemplating cutting up the orchard into half a dozen plots and perhaps we could buy one of them. I was still toying with the idea when Amala changed her mind and decided to sell the whole property and move south. She had even worked out a deal with the Sakya Monastery next door; but it fell through because the Sakyas backed off from the agreed price of thirty lakhs. And there it would have rested except that Harshad Mehta entered the picture.

From my father, each of us four children had inherited a large number of shares. Of these there were some eight hundred ACC shares, each valued at something more than their face value of Rs.100/- per share, which we split four ways. Then at some time, ACC offered us rights shares at Rs. 200 per share. The others indignantly rejected the offer as overpriced; and I had some spare money of Swamy's so I bought all the rights shares offered and so Swamy and I each had about 200 ACC shares. Over the years ACC went up a little and the others all sold their shares; and I had forgotten all about our 400 shares until one day, my share broker in Bombay phoned me up. Those were the days when Harshad Mehta was rocking the share world and he had decided to do something spectacular with ACC. My share broker phoned to say that ACC shares were trading for several thousand rupees a share and asked me whether I was interested in selling. "Of course," I said, stunned by the size of the appreciation, "Sell them at once."

My share broker diffidently said he thought the price would rise to Rs. 10,000;. "Well, okay," I said, awed, but greedy for this windfall, "But don't delay a day beyond Rs. 10,000/-".

So we sold our 400 shares for Rs. 10,000/- a share, netting a neat amount of some forty lakhs. It was just as well we sold when we did. Just days later, the shares tumbled quite as spectacularly as they had risen and ACC was back at Rs. 200/- per share, with hundreds, if not thousands of ruined speculators; but Swamy and I had a nest egg (after taxes) of some 32 lakhs.

Now we had enough money to match the Sakya offer; and I bought Amala's property for Rs. 31 lakhs.... As usual Swamy was the beneficiary quite painlessly...but if I thought he was going to use that lovely bungalow to inspire great works from his pen, I was sadly mistaken. So far Swamy has written some dozen books and some hundreds of articles; and most have been penned not in lovely Dehradun (he hardly manages the time to go there), but first in the windowless office Swamy built for himself in the Greater Kailash house (against my advice he refused the large lit picture window I had wanted and so had only himself to blame when the room went dark during the frequent Greater Kailash electricity blackouts) and later in the windowless basement office of our Nizamuddin home. I do not grumble too much because I at least enjoy our lovely Dehradun property with access to the nearby Reserve Forest.

Actually it proved a misnomer to call the Dehradun acquisition "painless". The sale by Swamy's aunt to us, was a strictly non-black-money deal, possibly the only such one in the area, so that the sale price was way and above the submitted prices of comparable plot sales in the area. And so the Dehradun Collectorate decided that it was very suspicious that we should have bought at such a high price. It started proceedings against us; it took several years for our lawyer to convince a later, rather more open-minded Collector that there could not possibly be any wrong doing or tax evasion in buying at a price considerably higher than other comparable sales. Tax proceedings in India can be quite ridiculous.

V

The third item I plan to give that confirmed Swamy in his "the goods of this world" thesis is our acquisitions in the automobile line.

In 1969, when we returned to India, Swamy bought a car, a four wheel Mahindra jeep, which because of the shape of its built up body, we called "the biscuit van"; we loaded a ten month old Gitanjali, a kerosene stove, my mother-in-law's gift of a Rukmani cooker (a Tamil variety of pressure cooker in which a billycan, a shallow saucepan and a deep saucepan are piled precariously one on top of the other on the kerosene stove to cook rice, dal and one veg, which process I never quite mastered), and headed south to the Madurai headquarters of J.P.s Gandhi Peace Foundation, and thereafter to a rural stay in Batlagundu. Swamy had vigorously opposed what he called the "unnecessary luxury" of a four-wheel drive, because he said he had no intention of ever getting off the tarred road system of India; but with memories of the cactus edged dirt tracks that my father used to drive us on in Gujarat, I held out for it.

Swamy proved right: in the eight years we owned the biscuit van we never once put that four wheel drive into action. But it was a good car with a rather rough ride and we did many Bharat Darshans in it.

In 1971, Lok Sabha elections were announced. By then Swamy though not yet a full time politician, was an ardent supporter of the Jan Sangh; so when our friend Hukumchand Kachwai looked longingly at the biscuit van and said it was just what he needed to campaign in in his constituency, Swamy could not turn a deaf ear to his pleas. I was a little appalled because apart from the inconvenience of being car-less for the duration of the elections, I had discovered that Hukumchandji's constituency comprehended the rougher portions of the Chambal Ravines; but anyway we handed it over. Hukumchandji spared no effort of man, beast or car in his election campaign and the biscuit van suffered in proportion. But it was a small consolation that in the general debacle suffered by non-Congress parties, one of the rosy highlights was that Hukumchandji at least got re-elected. We got back our biscuit van and rattled around in it anyway.

At that point, a good Samaritan appeared on the scene. It was Ram Nath Goenka owner of the Indian Express newspaper chain. He did not give us a new car; but one day he handed over to Swamy the spare key of his own, till then personally driven, Fiat, and said it was ours for as long as we wanted it. Ram Nathji kept the second key so that perhaps if he decided to take back the car, he could just walk in and drive it away. So we became a two car family.

In 1976, during the Emergency, to ensure that an absconding Swamy surrender to the Police, both the biscuit van and the Fiat, were impounded in the Hauz Khas Police Station; and since Swamy did not surrender, they remained there for the duration. The Fiat, returned to us after the end of the Emergency in 1977, was in fairly good shape; but the biscuit van, already a bit of a casualty after Hukumchandji's Chambal ravine handling, never recovered. Apparently it had been parked out at the Hauz Khas Police Station in the open so that anyone who needed a spring or a spark plug or a tyre simply helped themselves to that part of the biscuit van. Naturally after that sort of treatment, the biscuit van refused to function; so Swamy (now a member of the ruling parliamentary party) haughtily sent it back to the Police Station. They tinkered with it and sent it back to us. We tried it out again, were dissatisfied and sent it back. They tinkered again and sent it back. This back-and-forth routine went on for some months. Finally Swamy complained right at the top to the Home Minister Chaudhary Charan Singh; but even the Chaudhary's peremptory orders could not make that biscuit van function respectably. On the advice of our friend Prakash the IIT bus driver, (in picturesque Punjabi, he explained that the police had put it together again with spit and tape; so naturally everytime the spit dried the bits fell apart) we finally gave up on the biscuit van, took delivery from the Police and sold it for scrap.

But then yet another good Samaritan appeared, my brother-in-law Srikantan. As he did to everything he owned, Srikantan looked after his car, also a fiat, but called a Premier

Padmini, with meticulous care, duly changed the oil and the sparkplugs and other things with copybook precision and polished the paintwork to within an inch of its life; so the car was as good as new when Srikantan decided to get a newer Padmini. Of course, we were delighted to be gifted his earlier one; and so we passed on our earlier Fiat to a needy friend so that he could graduate from a two wheeler to a four wheeler.

So we were back to being a single car family: this was a bit inconvenient because by then I had joined the Bar and one car shared between Swamy and me meant that we had to do quite a lot of planning. In the morning Swamy would drop me off at the chamber of my senior Soli Sorabjee; and after early morning conferences there, I would hitch a ride to the Courts from one of my more fortunately placed fellow juniors, (each of whom had a second hand car of his own, carefully selected by a plutocrat parent with the contacts to get a good secondhand car deal) or even my senior Soli (naturally Soli's car did not need to be secondhand). During the day if any conveyance was necessary I would hail a taxi or a three wheeler "auto"; and in the late evening, an obliging Swamy would pick me up again.

It was not that we were so badly off that we could not have afforded a second (second hand) car: it was simply that in those days in India, good sturdy reliable second hand cars were not easily available (my fellow juniors, Harish and Anu, had the contacts to get the rare scarcely used second hand one); and I was simply unequipped to handle a stalled car on the road; and the only new car within our budget was the new Maruti, for which the waiting list ran into the lakhs.

So we were delighted when a kindly disposed Arun Nehru, a crony of Sanjay Gandhi and a Director of the Maruti Suzuki Company, offered us an out of turn allotment—yet another one of the "goods of this world" to fall into Swamy's outstretched hand. With the acquisition of our shiny green Maruti, we were once more a two car family.

But anyone who had an off the shelf Maruti, was the target of every needy friend; and Swamy found he could not resist the urgings of his dear friend and party worker from Lucknow, Karuna Shankar Vajpayee. Karuna Shankarji literally thrust a cheque for the Maruti in Swamy's reluctant hand, took the keys and drove our Maruti away to his home in Lucknow. We were once more a one car family.

But the goods of this world are always available to Swamy's outstretched hand. Another obliging friend, Jayant Malhoutra, lobbied with the owners of the Premier Fiat Factory; and insisted that it was going to be Swamy's birthday next month, and they must give yet another out of turn allotment of a Premier to Swamy in time for his birthday. It was a beautiful plum coloured affair; but what made it particularly appealing to Swamy (who by then had a chauffeur as well as a second car) was that it had a reading lamp in the back seat so Swamy could sit in the backseat luxuriously reading away while the car took him wherever he needed to go.

The history of our later divestment and acquisition of automobiles could go on and on; but I will mercifully desist, even though their acquisition too went to prove Swamy's two fold thesis that the goods of this world are to be acquired only to improve one's efficiency and efficacy and that when one genuinely needs something, one merely holds out one's hand and the Heavens drop in the required article.

Chapter VIII

SWAMY ENTERS POLITICS

I

Meanwhile in the years following his expulsion from IIT, Swamy developed a political career. It all started quite simply. To keep the home fires burning, he had planned to return to teach at Harvard which had offered him an Associate Professorship. But in 1974, elections to the U.P. Legislative Assembly came due; and Nanaji Deshmukh asked Swamy whether he would like to manage the elections to the four Lucknow seats.

As Swamy put it to me, "I would like to do something there before leaving India"; and though we were financially quite strapped, I agreed that he should have his stint in Lucknow.

Though Jan Sangh did not win any of the Lucknow seats, it was a heart warmingly successful campaign in building up our friendships in the Jan Sangh and in Swamy kindling Jan Sangh unity in those four seats (even now Swamy has cordial ties with his old Jan Sangh friends in Lucknow). After it was over, the two of us got into our jeep to drive back to Delhi and the children, and presumably to wind up matters to proceed to the U.S.A.

But it did not turn out like that. We reached Delhi to find that Nanaji and Lal Krishna Advani, then President of the Jan Sangh, had been trying to locate Swamy: the Party had decided to field Swamy for the Rajya Sabha, from U.P. So Swamy, (who had never dreamt of this reward, and so had not taken the elementary precaution to get himself registered as a voter in Lucknow) was sent back to Lucknow to get himself registered as a voter there.

It was by no means an easy registration. There were very few days before the voter rolls closed; and there were the usual Shia-Sunni riots in Lucknow, which made things even tighter. But the registration got done, Swamy stood for election and he got elected as one of the two Jan Sangh M.P.s from U.P. elected that year. Now Swamy was well and truly in politics–a political career that was to progress with so many ups and downs.

II

One thing that Swamy learnt in his early parliamentary career is how fliberty gibbet can be the journalist's (and the public's) span of interest. The Press—only now it is the Media—with the possible exception of the financial papers, is not interested in anything deep, but rather in what is picayune or sensational. The Jan Sangh Parliamentary Party was generous of its Parliament time slots to Swamy; so to start with, Swamy would deliver carefully researched speeches full of facts and figures on various topics, mostly economic, which he thought the Nation needed to be educated on; but we cannot discover that anyone other than the Official Parliament Reporters, the recording stenos, read them. Then one day, he hit pay dirt. He had discovered that the Prime Minister's daughter-in-law Sonia was registered and doing a brisk business as a life insurance agent. This was illegal because Sonia then was not an Indian citizen and therefore not entitled to do so. Worse still her business consisted in taking on the life insurance requirements of everyone in the Prime Minister's Office, which was grossly improper, particularly as she resided in the Prime Minister's house. So Swamy made a speech on the subject, the Congress members got up to loudly defend their ewe-lamb, (forty years later I discovered just after Swamy was reinducted this year into the Rajya Sabha, that they still have that rather ridiculous knee jerk reaction to anything connected to their First Family) the Press sat up and took notice and Swamy hit the headlines. The headlines were continued the following day when the Prime Minister herself got up in Parliament to announce that Sonia had given up her life insurance business. So Swamy, like Ram Manohar Lohia before him, had learnt his lesson: Lohia, with a doctorate from Berlin and the corresponding scholarship to make learned speeches, once famously stated that the best way to get attention in the Indian Parliament was to throw a shoe. So Swamy continued to make headlines though he never actually threw a shoe. Also I want to emphasize, he has never made a headline that he cannot back up with chapter and verse.

III

Swamy also settled in quite happily into the perks and privileges attached to a Parliament membership. Very early on he had discovered an unoccupied diwan hidden away in the reading room; and while he used it regularly for catnaps, he appears never to have been discovered or disturbed there. He continued to use it over his next four terms in parliament. When, after a long gap of a decade and a half (he was not elected after 1999), Swamy was nominated this year to the Rajya Sabha, one of his earliest concerns was to find out whether the diwan was still available and still undiscovered. He found to his dismay that the diwan had been shipped out to the new swish Parliament House Library: too far for him: he likes to be close to the action.

In those days before Operation Flood, milk was in perennial short supply in Delhi; and ordinary people like us got by with two or three tokens. So we were rather overwhelmed to discover that as an M.P., Swamy was entitled to 10 milk tokens. I started using them with gay abandon until our Greater Kailash neighbours came in a delegation to object. Apparently our 10 tokens were cutting into the entire Greater Kailash milk quota. Our neighbours did not want us to cut down on our supply; only could the M.P. Sahib increase the entire GK milk supply? Swamy discovered that a simple request to the Milk people accomplished that at once. So both us and GK were flooded with milk.....During the Emergency, after Swamy was expelled from Parliament, we lost our milk tokens. After the Emergency, when Swamy was back in office, he asked me whether I would like the milk tokens back. But by going underground during the Emergency, he had failed to keep abreast with developments in the milk supply line in

Delhi: there now was no longer a need to queue up for milk. There was plenty of milk, I assured him, and nobody needed to apply for milk tokens any more.

Another valuable perk of office is that a spouse is entitled to an air ticket/first class train fare from Delhi to the "normal place of residence in the constituency". The fare might not have been much; but oh the relief of not having to stand in day-long queues (which was the norm in those pre-computorised booking days), months in advance of a projected trip! I used the privilege lavishly; and since I did the bookings myself rather than use an assistant (most MP wives do not personally do their own bookings) I made quite a few respectful friends among the extremely courteous and obliging railway booking staff in the Railway Reservation Office in Parliament House. .... I still remember the last time I used the facility: it was in 1999: Parliament had been dissolved prematurely and Swamy had been among those instrumental in bringing down Vajpayee's second Government; and the powers that be naturally did not want to be particularly obliging to someone like that. They could not do anything about Swamy's own railway pass because it was a perquisite available for life. But some angry BJP supporter in the railway staff decided to make things difficult for Swamy's wife. Our assistant came back from the booking office to say that since I had delayed using the facility of the spouse ticket for return-to-constituency–after–Parliament-session (which for that parliament stint was Madurai), it was no longer available and I would have to personally pay for the return ticket, which I would have to queue up for like any other ordinary citizen. I could have lumped that; but, being a trained lawyer who thought she knew her rights, I chose to follow up the matter. I went across to the Parliament Railway Booking Office to point out that it was just possible that a spouse might be too poor to personally pay for the return fare she had counted on to get her home. Did that mean she would be stuck in Delhi for the rest of her life, or at least until she had saved up enough money to stand the fare? The Booking Clerk had no sense of humour. "I cannot help you Madam" he said coldly, "That is the rule." I suppose I could have followed it up to the Secretary General of the Lok Sabha; but I was too overawed to proceed to that. So this last trip was paid for by Swamy personally.

I must not forget to mention the major M.P. perquisite: "living accommodation", and provision for a rather modest electricity, water and telephone bill. As for the perquisite of a house, over the years we have worked our way through a slew of "living accommodations". The first-which we never personally occupied/consisted of three Vithalbhai Patel House suites: two of these were used as the Jan Sangh office (a far cry from the present palatial premises of the BJP, stretching to bungalows and outhouses covering several acres) and the third was used by my sister Coomi, her husband and her baby. It was an ideal introduction to Parliament people, since so many Opposition M.P.s or their workers lived there; in the first couple of years we got to know a huge number of them (which proved quite useful for communication during the ensuing Emergency years, when many Vithalbhai Patel House flats harboured absconders and others wanted by the Law).

We lost the rooms in Vithalbhai Patel House when Swamy was expelled from the Rajya Sabha in 1976; but a year later we were back in the New Delhi area. This time as a second-term M.P., Swamy got a huge nightmare of a bungalow, constructed in the 1920s, originally for the "native members" of the Viceroy's Council. It had twelve rooms (many of them converted verandahs or windowless "zenana" inner rooms, suitable doubtless for the zenanas that the 1920s "native members" brought with them), a football field sized courtyard presumably for the retainers and cattle that the "native members" naturally brought with them, an antediluvian brick-work kitchen that must have suited the half dozen khansamas the "native member" must have employed to feed his retinue, and bathrooms done up with the fittings considered up-to-date for the "native members" of the 1920s. The ancient walls were riddled with tunnels built over the decades by hordes of happy rats and mongooses: I can remember a visiting Chinese Ambassador watching petrified as a rather large rat strolled across the drawing room floor and disappeared into his tunnel where no doubt his family awaited him. My English sister-in-law got her chic boots chewed up by another monster, because she had fecklessly left them on her bedroom floor. The wiring was all surface, nailed to the walls on wooden planking, which suited the rats as they would practice acrobatic expeditions on the ceilings and walls (our dog would sit around below the wiring just in case a rat wobbled and fell down when he could snap it up). The children had to be escorted into the lofty bathrooms and their hands held because they were terrified of the lizards darting around on the high ceilings: I recall a small Chu heaving a sigh of relief when introduced to a railway toilet because, as she explained, she could use it without having to keep her eyes fixed on the ceiling, for a possible falling lizard.

So you see there was plenty of animal life in No. 22 Rajendra Prasad Road; and since the animal rights version of Maneka Gandhi had not yet appeared on the scene to terrorise us into tenderly looking after them, we did not hesitate to keep rat traps all over the place and to encourage our dog to capture and kill them…This did not always happen simply because a tenderhearted Kamal Singh used to cycle down to India Gate and release the rats there…. There was wild life in the large walled garden too: the occasional scorpion would drop from the ancient trees.

Also there were no damp courses, so after the rains, the damp crept up the walls and the whitewash peeled off onto the floor. M.P.s in those days were simple Gandhian servants of the people so people put up with these homes, unlike the present breed of spoilt M.Ps who insist on improvements like landscape windows, granite flooring and ceilings lowered for airconditioning. (I believe one plutocrat M.P. has even installed a retractable glass ceiling, which of course I would love to appropriate; but unfortunately no one has offered it to us). But there were any number of servants quarters (a blessing we had not experienced in our earlier homes) and the walled garden was large and sunny and I started my gardening career there.

On the whole, we were happy to move onto less antiquated accommodation, when as third term, fourth term and fifth term M.P., Swamy got more modern homes, beautifully appointed and with a curiously identical floorplan (almost identical indeed to Swamy's present accommodation as a sixth term M.P.). You may well ask why the same house would not just have been continued with all along. That is because in between stints as M.P., there would be periods out of office, when we would pack up our belongings and move back to Greater Kailash. It meant quite a lot of to-ing and fro-ing along the highway from India Gate to Greater Kailash, with carloads of chinaware and pictures which we could not leave to the tender mercies of the truckers. Gitanjali, who at one time was addicted to Scottish folklore, would describe our journeys in terms of travelling over, "the seven bens and seven glens and seven mountain moors", like the King of Scotland's daughter.

Finally when Swamy became a Minister, we got a truly elegant bungalow with "Grecian" pillars (I think such bungalows are called "Type VIII" which is as high as you can get in the PWD housing hierarchy). I was not very enthusiastic about moving in because I expected that Swamy's stint as a Minister, would be quite shortlived and then we would be shifted back to our humbler "Type VII-AB"; but actually we continued in it until Swamy's term expired (it was a Rajya Sabha term, so it extended for six years). We had got Gitanjali married from this Type VIII house (the size of the lawns allowed us to invite almost the entire Supreme Court Bar Association) and I was hoping to hold onto it for a month beyond our entitlement because Chu was getting married; but though the then Prime Minister, our friend H.D. Deve Gowda was quite willing to oblige, our humble request was turned down by a Government officer who sent a stiff refusal, asking us "to kindly co-operate" in an early vacation of the premises. It was such a humiliating denial that I straight away packed our bags and moved out; so Chu was married from our Greater Kailash home; and the reception could be held in large style only because her in-laws the Haidars kindly made their own "accommodation" available (Salman Haidar was then Foreign Secretary and that post has a large dedicated modern bungalow and garden). Both our daughters are married into bureaucratic families; and I think both these families were rather wary about mixing with "political" types. Certainly Gitanjali's in-laws (her father in law was then Union Expenditure Secretary) decided that rather than host a joint reception to which all "those politicians" would come, they would hold their own smaller more exclusive bureaucratic one.

But the Type VIII was truly huge and could have housed an army. The family rooms were large and numerous and when we moved in, it had attached to it, fourteen servants quarters, most of them occupied by a family of cowherds and their cows, (the previous allottee was obviously a gau rakshak) which it took the Housing Department several months to evict.

The Type VIII had acres of garden, including a sunken garden which I tried desperately but ineffectually to landscape with a series of lily pools (after that whenever we moved we would dig up the cement lily pools and carry them to our next garden....so our progress across Delhi was marked by large gaping pits). There, partridges roosted in the bushes awaking us each morning with their delightful "racket" (that was the unpoetic Swamy's description of these joyful sounds); also lapwings which were silly enough to nest in open holes in the lawn, which the dogs would winkle out; also one solitary owlet which regular as clockwork, would occupy the same branch at twilight when it hunted for mice.

There were rose bushes and Raat Ki Rani bushes by the dozens: one can delight in six or seven bushes, but dozens are difficult to handle or appreciate. There was an enormous vegetable garden where in the beginning the mali and I tried to grow seasonal vegetables like cabbages and cauliflowers. But, I discovered that cabbages and cauliflowers all grow at the same rate and become ready for consumption around the same time; so there would be days when we had several dozen cabbages/cauliflowers at the same time, and we could not eat our way through all that or even give them away to friends. In desperation I took to growing potatoes and onions, which can be stored; but neither my gardener nor I mastered the art of growing premium grade crops: year after year our potatoes were small and tended to rot if we kept them for any length of time. So then I tried growing maize; but as the crop ripened, hordes of parrots would descend to eat up the whole crop. Curiously (unlike the situation today in Lutyens Delhi) there were no monkeys around in those days, so we were saved that invasion. Finally I experimented with asparagus; but asparagus plants take a dozen years to mature; and by that time, we were out of the Type VIII bungalow: I have sometimes wondered whether our successor there, ex-

President Venkatraman, enjoyed our asparagus….. I do not need to inform you that Swamy took not the slightest interest in our horticultural efforts, just as he took no interest in the rich bird life.

One small bonus I got from that house were the fireplaces. We did not light fires in them; but I did discover that my tulip bulbs which used to dry out and perish in storage in the Delhi summers, stayed alive if you pushed a sack of bulbs up the chimney stack and kept them there through the summer.

But I am now wandering very far afield from Swamy's first term as M.P. In those days, access to the Parliament House grounds too, was quite relaxed. At one time, we lived on Rajendra Prasad Road quite close to Parliament House, so on holidays, Swamy would take his dog walking through the Parliament House grounds, entering at one end and exiting at Vijay Chowk; and no one ever stopped them. Our dog soon discovered his favourite spots there for relieving himself.

I too enjoyed those early years in Parliament, tagging on with Swamy in a way I have never done since. Everyone—M.P.s, Officers, Peons, Watch and Ward staff—knew everyone else and was friendly and kindly; and once you were recognised as a frequenter you could go about anywhere largely unchecked: the Emergency and later terrorism threats changed all that. But while it lasted it was a wonderfully warm place to be in.

For one thing the library there was magnificent. This was not the present separate library which is impressive, and comprehensive and a rather underutilised soul-less art-piece; but the historic pre-independence one which occupied much of the upper reaches of the main Parliament building and looked as if it had been much used in the days of the Constituent Assembly. (Naturally it specialised in things politic and legal and administrative but I discovered to my delight that it did not turn up its nose at Agatha Christie). There was a grand Reading Room for newspapers and magazines on the ground floor which was much frequented by Hon'ble Members (where as I told you a few paragraphs ago, Swamy found his catnap cubbyhole); but for me the fascinating parts were on higher floors. This was many roomed, overflowing with books (these had overflowed into all the winding corridors and winding staircases all around the building) and crammed with racks round which you had to steer yourself and hope you were going in the right direction. While there was a well prepared staff just dying to be used, as far as I can recall in my pre-Emergency days there, there were only a few regular users like L.K. Advani, Madhu Dandavate, Mahavir Tyagi, Meenakshi Gopinath (later Principal of Lady Sri Ram College) and me. (The occasional privileged journalist would sometimes pop in but most journalists preferred cups of tea and gossip in Central Hall). You could find the most unprocurable old journals there and if you wanted could even get yourself inducted into the rotunda and watch the proceedings from high above if you did not mind the bees and (I think but I am not sure) the bats. Later in my early days at the Bar, I earned some reputation in Court because I unearthed a complete set of Hansard in the rotunda, which Mr. H.M. Seervai, Senior Counsel, needed to refer to: the ancient volumes were too fragile for photostatting, so I wore myself out, copying them out.

Swamy too enjoyed those early years, and was thrilled to meet ancient veterans including Founding Fathers of the Constitution and members of the early Lok Sabhas and Rajya Sabhas. There was a lot of friendly discussion with Parliamentarians of every hue, Congress, Jan Sanghi, Socialist, Communist, Gandhian and Anarchist: it was just one large strong viewed, close minded club, and everyone welcomed Swamy and allowed him to hold forth.

At that point Swamy's success in Parliament was short-lived only for lack of the time to develop it. Within some two years of his election, the Emergency was declared; Swamy who had a warrant for his arrest, went underground; and the rest of us settled into the long haul of living in uncertain and financially precarious times.

Chapter IX

EARLY DAYS OF THE EMERGENCY

I

We learnt of the Emergency at some unearthly hour like two o'clock in the morning of the 25th June 1975. The phone rang and the disembodied voice at the other end asked Swamy whether he was there, adding that if he was, they "were coming to get him". Swamy was startled. The previous night there had been a huge public meeting at Ram Lila Grounds; and Swamy had been there sitting between Morajibhai and JP, (they did not get on well with each other) with Nanaji's instructions to keep the peace between them; but he had not anticipated anything like this. While he was wondering about his next move, the phone rang again: this time it was Sundari Malkani, wife of K.R. Malkani, the editor of the Party's newspaper "Motherland" to tell us that the police had just taken Malkani away. So Swamy decided to make himself scarce. As dawn arose, Swamy drove away, startling a few shadowy persons who had been hanging around outside. In a few days he had rendezvoused with what was left unimprisoned of the Central Jan Sangh leadership. And he had the car sent back to me.

For the first few months of the Emergency, Swamy moved around India with Nanaji Deshmukh, (who was organising the RSS Underground) acting as his driver. Nanaji till then a respectable dhoti clad gentleman with greying hair, now emerged as a bespectacled business man in a grey safari suit and dyed black hair. And Swamy became a Sardarji. It was a pretty convincing disguise; and it became quite well known later after the Emergency was over, because at one time while he was hiding out in my sister Coomi's apartment (Coomi, her husband and baby were then occupying the Vithalbhai Patel House apartment allotted to Swamy as an M.P.), Coomi took a photograph of him so disguised.

Later Coomi regretted having so photographed him: the photograph was taken in her bathroom, with a geyser in the background and Coomi lived in mortal fear that the Police would actually recognise and pinpoint the geyser and locate and book her: it did not happen: the photograph was never discovered by the Police. In fact, a matter for some amusement, after the hunt for Swamy was well and truly on, the Police confiscated and took away a photograph of Shri Sai Baba that used to adorn my sister-in-law Sushila's bureau, under the impression that that was Swamy in disguise.

For the hounded Underground in the early days of the Emergency, there were just two safe havens in India–Gujarat where the Nav Nirman agitation had brought an anti-Congress government into existence (indeed this had precipitated the declaration of Emergency) and Tamil Nadu which had an anti-Congress DMK Government. So in the first few months, often it was there that Swamy gravitated and made deep and lasting contacts with politicians (local and refugee, Jan Sangh, Congress (O), Swatantra Party, PSP, SSP and DMK) he would otherwise never have met and bonded with. Surprisingly, considering how bad their relationship is now, Karunanidhi befriended him. Swamy also spent time in Bombay feasting on bhel puris among the Gujjus at Chowpatty. Often he would catch a train to Gujarat. All Gujarat bound trains slowed down near Daman –to facilitate the smugglers who would enter or detrain at that point; and Swamy would clamber in or out along with the smugglers. In Ahmadabad, he made a contact which would have commanded a glamorous rolodex entry forty years later: he would be received and looked after by a dedicated Swayam Sevak he had known since 1972, on whose motorbike he would ride to visit the Jan Sangh minister Makarand Desai. And while discussing more serious matters, the three of them would motorcycle down to an icecream stall to enjoy the humble treat of a fruit icecream for which Ahmadabad was famous. Forty years later the humble Swayam Sevak became the Prime Minister of India. Whenever Swamy met us during the Emergency, he would wax lyrical on those Ahmadabad fruit icecreams; but I don't remember his ever having mentioned the facilitator of those humble treats, Shri Narendrabhai Modi. Of course, perhaps that may have been to protect Narendrabhai's Emergency incognito.

While he was doing the organising, Nanaji was a regular dynamo, who managed to find some use or other for any volunteer. For example, because I happened to have a valid unexpired passport, I was dispatched to the U.S. and the U.K. to establish communications with sympathisers there. As far as my RSS contacts there were concerned, it was just a question of telling them that a Resistance existed, which they would assist and foster through their usual channels; and I may mention that RSS people like our wonderful friend Jatinder who has never deserted us since even in our most alienated-from-RSS days, did a wonderful job of organising and publishing meetings and protests. As far as Swamy's Harvard and MIT ex-colleagues were concerned they expressed sympathy for Swamy but their encouragement extended largely to promising to actively protest if and when Swamy were arrested. Our personal friends abroad were more individualistic and imaginative. For instance Satish Singh was training himself to relay messages in Morse on an underground radio system (it would perhaps have been useful if we had ever set up such an underground radio, but we never did); Meera Mitra in Pennsylvania (her husband, a student of Swamy's at Delhi University and later a colleague at IIT, went on some 40 years later, to become the Finance Minister of West Bengal) worked out a code to be used in sending letters to and from us: Meera would disguise them as cooking recipes and I would reply with more cooking recipes; and Zerbanoo Gifford started cultivating all the rather bewildered Gujarati residents of her neighbouring Harrow-on-the-Hill.

Very soon after my return, Nanaji was discovered in a raid, and arrested and so for the rest of the Emergency, he was in Tihar jail. Since my brother-in-law Virendra was there too, we used to meet him (unlike the criminal accused, we could actually mingle with the detenus). This was on Visitor's Days, which turned out to be quite festive occasions. All the relations of political detenues would turn up in their best clothes, bearing hampers of delicacies which were generously shared out. The most disagreeable feature was the state of the jail loos; but that was not just the complaint of us visitors: the detenus loudly deplored them. Years later when the present government decided to honour Emergency heroes, one enterprising minister wanted the honour to be restricted only to those who had actually been in jail (in which case of course, Swamy would be out of consideration for that honour) and one suspects that he must have had the jail loos in mind. Unfortunately for his vision, the Prime Minister himself having spent the Emergency years underground had not experienced those jail toilets, and so possibly he did not find the Honourable Minister's suggestion, a reasonable classification. So to the enterprising minister's chagrin, last year Swamy got decorated as an Emergency "hero".

As for Swamy, he went abroad using an unusual take-off by air flight from Trichinopoly to Colombo, cooling his heels in Colombo until the next flight to London, (to his dismay it took quite long to come during which time he had nothing to maintain himself on except his American Express Credit Card), and then on to the West, where he travelled extensively trying to educate people on the tyrannies of the Emergency Government. One remarkably open minded and hospitable person there was Swamy's old friend B.K. Nehru (a former colleague of Daddy, whom

Swamy had known when as Ambassador in Washington he would visit Harvard for talks). He was now our High Commissioner in the U.K. and when Swamy phoned him up, he insisted on inviting the proscribed Swamy to tea….. there were unusually courageous and gentlemanly persons like that!

However in general Swamy's foreign activities upset Indira Gandhi, who objected to anyone abroad learning unfavourable aspects of the Emergency, or indeed that there was some sort of resistance at all, kept alive in India; so finally we started getting a tougher police surveillance. For one week, the newspapers and radio broadcast the (to me) humiliating news that Dr. Subramanian Swamy M.P. was going to be prosecuted under the Contravention of Foreign Exchange and Prevention of Smuggling Activities Act. The general public would be pardoned for thinking that Swamy was involved in some smuggling and foreign exchange racket: but actually the charge against him was simply that having gone abroad on a few months' permission, he had stayed on there without further permission (under our stringent foreign exchange act, even such an overstay was a criminal offence). We also suffered a police camp outside our house and a police tail.

Under these conditions, the rest of the family (myself, the two children and my sister-in-law Sushila and the cook Parvati) settled into our home in Greater Kailash. There we were bunkered in for the duration of the Emergency, with (as I narrated earlier) fortunately a roof over our head and furniture and a fridge and a cook still in residence. We even had an income to run the home fires because even though shortly thereafter Swamy was expelled from the Rajya Sabha and lost his salary, the Government procedures did not provide for cutting off the pension that all ex-MPs get. It was small but we got by.

So I did not need to go out and earn a living-(i.e. assuming anyone wanted to hire me—I had in any case, long ago, lost my Mathematics fellowship at the IIT, and the Jan Sangh Weekly "Organiser", to which I contributed a weekly article, (culled with the help of the Parliament House Library facilities) had been closed down by the government at the outset of the Emergency)—so I could settle down to a three year Law Course at Delhi University. (My admission there was facilitated by Om Prakash Tyagi, one of the very few Jan Sangh M.P.s who was not in jail, and so could give me the requisite certificate, required by Delhi University, stating, "She bears a good moral character"). Of course there was no car (both cars had been attached); so I had to take a bus to College; but then so did every other student. The only difference was that while I travelled by bus to the University, the bus was followed by a carload of Police gum shoes tracking my every move. There was a lighter side to this cavalcade as I realised when the couple sitting behind me in the bus noticed this. "How strange!", the girl said, "Every time the bus halts, there is a car behind it which also halts; and then starts up when the bus starts up." The bus route was pretty long: Lady Sree Ram College-Lodhi Road Market-Central Secretariat-Tilak Marg-Red Fort-Civil Lines-the University; and by the end of the Emergency the Police Escort must have been heartily sick of following that route, halting en route, to and fro, week after week. But then it was not an object with me to make life pleasant for my escort.

It was not only I who had this escort: the children, the cook, my sister-in-law, my brother-in-law, my sister...I wonder whether the tax payer knows how his hard won taxes can be utilised by a vengeful Government with an apparently unlimited Police Budget. I hated my escort and haughtily disdained to notice them let alone smile at them. The cook was rude and aggressive and anti-police, (Swamy used to joke that she must have come from a long line of Ratnagiri smugglers) and loudly accused them of shadowing an unprotected female for base reasons; my sister-in-law Sushila was pleasant and cheerful, and even suggested that her escort give her a ride (they did not); but from their point of view the nicest was my brother-in-law (a film buff) who consulted their taste as to which movies he should go and see. He paid for his cinema ticket; and the tickets of the carload of policemen no doubt were paid for by the tax payer.

II

There was never any letup in the Police vigilance. After all every month they had to appear before their bosses to explain why another month had passed without their producing Dr. Subramanian Swamy. I remember one momentous series of raids in May 1976, which occurred while I was in Bombay helping to arrange for my father's trip to the U.S. for treatment of his cancer of the liver. The Enforcement Directorate raided his Bombay house where, to save my parent's further harassment, I handed over my letters from Swamy. (At that time I did not see the funny side of the matter: the police kept apologising to Daddy for the liberty they were taking in raiding the home of an ex-I.C.S. boss).

They raided our Delhi house too. Two of our friends, both at the thesis writing stage had asked if they might spend a few quiet days there. But it was anything but quiet. The whole house was gone through with a tooth comb; our chor khana was unerringly plundered by the Enforcement Directorate; and every scrap of paper was carried away to be deciphered. My poor archaeologist friend Sherene Ratnagar had to spend several days thereafter quietly knitting in order to get back a peaceful frame of mind; and the other occupant, Raiomond Irani (who had camped at our place only so he could use our electric typewriter which had the facility of Greek and Hebrew mathematical symbols) lost a good bit of his I.I.T. thesis calculations.

Mr. Narasimhan, who was then editor of the Financial Express and should know about matters like that, told me that the Enforcement Directorate were looking for shady foreign exchange transactions; so every numeral in the confiscated papers had to be analysed just in case it referred to some foreign exchange. For example if a letter referred to 25 apples, it would be analysed to figure out if these apples were really apples and not lakhs of dollars. Since by training Swamy is a mathematical economist and I am a mathematician, there was no dearth of numbers for the Enforcement Directorate to cut its teeth on, even if Raiomond's thesis in engineering had not been there to complicate matters further. Eventually, in disgust they called me over to decipher at least Swamy's letters. Now these letters included a full scale disguised plan for his return to India in August; so I had a field day falsely reading all the clues to wean them away from any hint of Swamy's projected return.

Chapter X

SWAMY RETURNS TO INDIA

I

And that return was the next highlight of our lives. To keep their membership alive, Parliamentarians are required to be present in the House at least once every six months. Since quite a few Members had been jailed (the polite word used by the Government, was "detained"), and so could not be present in Parliament, Parliament had developed the practice of routinely granting leave of absence to any M.P. who applied for it; and in that way Swamy too had been routinely granted leave of absence. But of course, once he had become a pest abroad, the Government tightened the screws and refused to grant him further leaves, and the time was approaching when he would forfeit his membership by these absences. It was Swamy's plan to enter India, appear in the Rajya Sabha, record his presence and then vanish if he could. To all our surprise he actually managed just that.

Swamy had planned it with meticulous care. Earlier we had done some fancy fiddling with the idea of getting him to Kathmandu and his then entering India through the footpaths and mountain routes of Western Nepal; but we soon realised that that might take several aeons to negotiate. Swamy might end up like the White Russians who worked their way through Siberia, only to find that the World War they were to extend to the east coast, had got over several years earlier.

So entry would have to be by air. It was not so easy because the Government had someone tailing Swamy, then in the U.K.. Fortuitously, some genuine Swamyji, was then organising a camp in Scotland; and the British newspapers carried the news that the Swamy was in Scotland. Our Swamy's tail thought it was he who had gone to Scotland, and they relaxed their vigilance a bit. A slot for Swamy to leave the U.K. without being followed, thus opened up.

Also it would not be a good idea to travel on a false name and passport—a crime under all ordinary international law. Since all Passenger Manifests were scrutinised for travellers actually entering India, Swamy decided to buy a ticket to Bangkok on a flight which would stop to refuel on Indian soil and board and deboard only such passengers as were on the Manifest for India: so his name, (he had bought a ticket for Bangkok), did not appear in the Passenger Manifest for India. Then once landed along with a transit Pass for the Airport Waiting Area, Swamy edged his way into the stream of deboarding passengers. His egress was helped by the fact that that night there were a lot of sports enthusiasts who had come to welcome home a winning football team. When a sleepy policeman stopped him, Swamy simply produced his Rajya Sabha pass, the policeman saluted him and let him through….and Swamy was on Indian soil.

He walked to the cabstand, (which in those days was just outside the Airport Exit Door) hopped a cab upto near Greater Kailash and then walked again upto our home. There was a posse of policemen guarding the entrance but they must have been pretty relaxed in the dark hours because no one noticed him walk in and rap lightly on my bedroom window; and I let him in.

We talked and talked and then Swamy suggested we pack up the children, get into the car, and register at a hotel as an out of town family going to visit the Taj Mahal. So that's what we did. As usual Gitanjali suddenly discovered that she didn't want to miss school. She went along protesting; but eventually she only missed one school day. The RSS underground, when told of the plan, vetoed it because when our police escort found all of us missing, they might well track Swamy down along with us. So after a very short sojourn and a lavish breakfast at Hotel Rajdoot, the RSS arranged instead for Swamy to be put up in a Party worker's house, and the kids and I returned home.

But Swamy felt he could jeopardise the Party worker and his family just in case the Police raided them and found him there. He decided that the only safe place where no one would be prosecuted in case he was found out, was in his own house. So shortly thereafter, Swamy (who had already fixed that with me) got back into his home by getting into his Sardarji outfit, presenting himself at the house gate and simply stating to the police posse guarding our entrance that he had come to repair the TV. By the time the posse changed they had already forgotten to recheck out the TV repairman. So Swamy stayed in his own home for the next few days.

It was by no means a quiet interlude. My sister Coomi who was told of his plan, visited him to give him a lecture on how his hare-brained scheme would imperil the rest of us. Then our friend Satish Singh (he lived in the U.S. and had arrived now just to be in on the kill) settled in with Swamy in the back bedroom (the two of them spent all the days discussing politics so no one was bored). Then my brother-in-law's Probation Officer turned up, (Virendra had been released from jail on parole and had given my address as his place of residence while on parole, so we had to phone him up to present himself there); and I was kept busy producing cups of tea for the Probation Officer while waiting for Virendra to come and record his presence: a not very comfortable situation when there is a Police officer in the drawing room and a wanted absconder in the back bedroom. Meanwhile the children too settled into the back bedroom. They were very good about not telling anyone about Swamy's presence. By then Chu was three years old and Gitanjali was seven and both took a fugitive father in the back bedroom as a matter of course. The other occupants of the house, my sister-in-law Sushila and the cook too took it in their stride.

In the next few days among my other chores, was the job of going to Parliament, (in those days you could park your car-if it had a parliamentary sticker-inside the Parliament House Compound and a simple Member's Spouse Identification Card was all that was required to enter the building), enter through a Side Gate near the

Rajya Sabha, and carefully measure the number of steps and the time it would take to walk upto the Rajya Sabha entrance door and out again to the car park.

Four days later a washed, brushed and shaved Swamy in kurta pajama got into the car with me and we drove out of the driveway too rapidly for it to register with the police posse that here again was the TV repairman but not in Sardarji kit. Swamy dropped me at the Church of the Redemption next door to Rashtrapati Bhavan; and himself drove to Parliament, parked the car close to the Rajya Sabha Entrance point, and entered the building. The Watch and Ward Staff recognised him and saluted him so he didn't even need to show any identification.

I was the backup: in case Swamy was chased, he would drive to the Church of the Redemption, hand over the car to me and hoof it from there while I drove the car back into view of the Police. In case no such chase occurred Swamy would drive the car to Birla Mandir, park the car there and leave me to collect it.

I had a long and nervous wait outside the Church. People were walking up and down the road; and I felt that all eyes were focussed on me; and that these people were wondering suspiciously just what I was doing lingering there. Actually, it was August, jamun season in Delhi; and passers-by were mostly looking up at the trees wondering whether they would be lucky enough to get a ripe jamun to eat, or unlucky enough to have it splatter their clothes.

Swamy, his father and siblings with K. Kamaraj at their home, 1948

oxna's parents with her maternal grandparents and her uncle (who in Chapter III, arned the epithet of "butler" from Morarji bhai), at their ancestral home Dastur Hall, une, 1937.

Roxna's paternal grandparents and their family at their Poona home, taken after her navjote ceremony 1948. Roxna's father is second from the left, standing; her mother is second from the right, seated; and Roxna is first from the left, on the carpet.

Lowell House Faculty at Harvard 1964. Swamy is the fourth person in the second row.

Swamy and Roxna on the banks of the Charles River, Cambridge 1965.

Swamy and Roxna at their marriage ceremony June 10, 1966.

Swamy and Roxna, 1966.

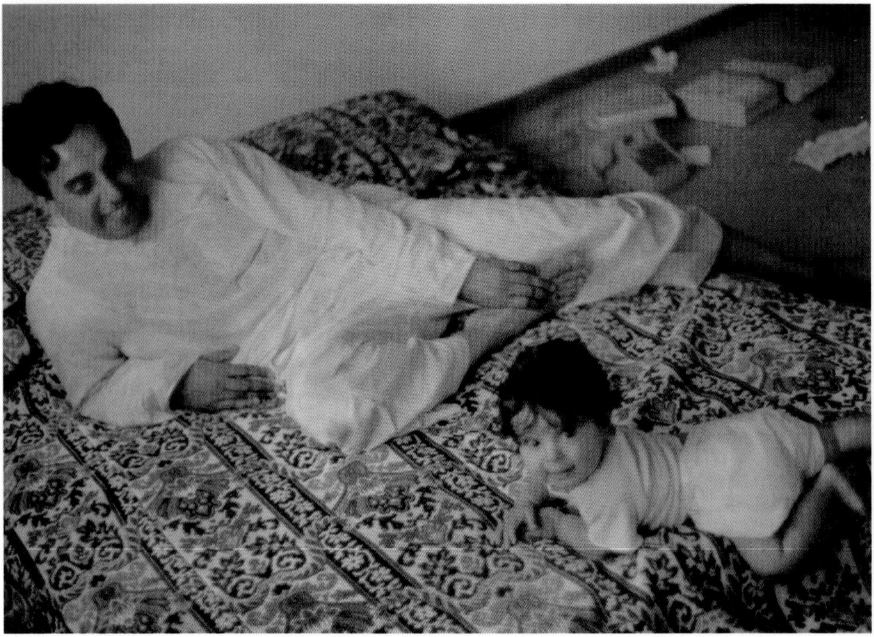

Swamy with Gitanjali, August 1969.

Swamy with Gitanjali aged 4 and Suhasini less than a month, February 1973.

Suhasini in 1975, just days before the Declaration of Emergency.

Vajpayee presiding over a seminar, at which he disagreed with Swamy, November 3, 1970.

Swamy, with JP, Morarjibhai, Nanaji Deshmukh and Raj Narain, June 24th, 1975.

Swamy in disguise as a Sardar, August-September 1975.

Swamy, a fugitive in Leicester, U.K.1976.

Swamy, the morning after his election victory, March 1977.

Raj Ghat Oath Taking Ceremony of Janata Party M.P.s, May 1977. (Swamy is just behind orajibhai; and Vajpayee is second from right in the front line).

Swamy and family, Madras, June 1977.

Swamy at a seminar presided over by P.M. Morarjibhai, June 1977.

Gitanjali, Suhasini and Winny, 1977.

Roxna and Swamy, Patna 1978.

Roxna and Swamy at an Arab Embassy reception 1978.

Swamy with J.P., June 1979.

The family with Winny at our second Parliamentary "accommodation" No. 16 Rajendra Prasad Road.

The family at our third Parliamentary "accommodation" No. 5 Purana Quila Road.

Swamy receives the Man of the Match Cup, from Indira Gandhi, November 1980.

Swamy at a meeting with Teng Tsaio Ping, Beijing April 1981.

Roxna and Children with Swamy's mother, Bangalore 1983.

Swamy with Sant Jarnail Singh Bhindranwala, Amritsar, October 1983.

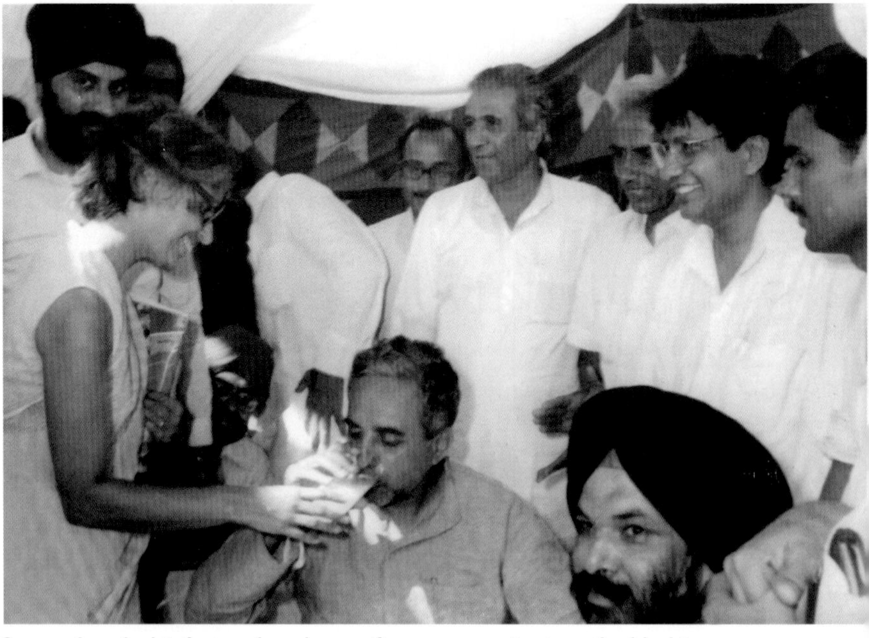

Swamy breaks his fast undertaken to force an enquiry into the Hashimpura massacres, Delhi 1988.

Swamy with P.M. Chandrashekhar at Rajghat, November 19, 1990.

Swamy and Roxna in Roxna's study, 1991.

Our "Type VIII" accommodation, No. 5 Safdarjang Road.

Swamy with P.M. P.V. Narasimha Rao,1995.

Swamy, once more at Harvard, July 1995.

Swamy and family with P.M. Deve Gowda at Suhasini's wedding reception, Delhi, September 1996.

Dr. Manmohan Singh releases Swamy's book "India's Labour Standards and the W.T.O. Framework", Delhi 2000.

The extended family at Abha Kapoor's wedding, Delhi, December 2003.

Swamy and Roxna with their children and grandchildren, Delhi, December 2003.

Swamy and Roxna with Tara, Hyderabad, December 2003.

Roxna and her three grand daughters Ava, Maya and Tara, Delhi January 2007

Chapter XI

SWAMY SETS THE JUMNA ON FIRE

I

Meanwhile, Swamy managed his appearance and disappearance from the Rajya Sabha. Apparently as he entered the Rajya Sabha Lobby, a Communist colleague Inderjit Gupta greeted him thinking no doubt that Swamy had been let out bonafide after signing the Twenty Point Programme. So Swamy entered with him just as the Chairman Vice President Jatti was reading out the obituaries which are the first item on the Agenda when Parliament reconvenes. The Police hovering around also recognised Swamy; but before confronting him, they decided to check out his actual status by making a few phone calls, (there is always a dread of having mishandled an Hon'ble Member of Parliament, when you might be hauled up before the Chairman for having committed the crime of obstructing the Hon'ble Member while he was doing his duty of representing the People).

It was a bad decision: in those days phone calls were notoriously difficult to effect and while they were struggling with the instrument Swamy managed an interjection in the House:

> Swamy: Mr. Speaker: Point of Order: you have made a notable omission in your Obituary References: you have left out Democracy from your list of the deceased".
> Mr. Jatti: "No. No point of Order is to be recorded",
> Swamy: "I am walking out in protest."

I should mention that the Chairman had the above dialogue entirely deleted so now it is not on the Records. But it is true nonetheless.

Throughout this exchange, the rest of the members, who had of course recognised Swamy, sat or stood frozen. The Minister of State for Home, Om Mehta, probably thinking that Swamy was about to throw a bomb, dived under his desk and stayed there. And Swamy, having made his point of order, walked out into the lobby where he saw the hapless Police still trying to get information over the telephone, got into his car, drove unchecked to Birla Mandir, left the car there with the key under the mat for me, (remember we had only one key because Ram Nath Goenka had held onto the other), and hailed a rickshaw to New Delhi Railway Station.

In his white pajama kurta and Gandhi topi, he easily passed for a Congress goon (there was a big jamboree to celebrate Quit India Day and the netas were all streaming out to catch their trains home), got into a Mathura bound train, and settled into the upper berth. No one disturbed him except the ticket collector. He was shown Swamy's ubiquitous Rajya Sabha pass and saluted and left Swamy in peace.

II

At Mathura Swamy got out, sent me the agreed on cable "Book published", and caught a south bound train to Nagpur, then changed to yet another train this time to Bombay, where he landed up at the doorstep of Ved Prakash Goyal, (who two decades later became Union Minister for Shipping) and into the delirious arms of the RSS.

It had been agreed with RSS leaders that for his return to India and his appearance in the Rajya Sabha, Swamy was on his own: had he been apprehended in the attempt with the connivance of the RSS underground, he might have imperilled their whole network. But Madhav Rao Mule had promised that once Swamy was clear and in Bombay, looking after him would be the Sangh's responsibility. They had appointed Ved Prakash Goyal's home as the rendezvous; and as soon as they got to know of Swamy's Rajya Sabha appearance, a man had been posted to linger outside Ved Prakashji's home to look out for the fugitive.

For the RSS it was the only bright spot in a gloomy underground. So whoever in the top Bombay based RSS brass was not in jail, turned up at an extremely emotional meeting in a Vile Parle residence, where the RSS took over the responsibility of keeping Swamy safe in hiding. For months, they had lived on the edge of despair: till then nothing seemed to be moving against the entrenched Government; and now Swamy had bearded the lion in its own den and escaped too.

And the icing on the cake was that the whole world knew of it. Of course the Government saw to it that nothing about Swamy's escapade appeared in the Indian newspapers; but of course the underground Press and the gossip from man to man ensured that his exploit was common knowledge among the disaffected in India.

Besides, a day before the event, I had visited a contact in the Australian Broadcasting Corporation posted in Delhi; and suggested that he might find it worthwhile to cover the Rajya Sabha proceedings next day. He got the hint and alerted the whole foreign Press–with the result that that day, the Press Gallery in the Rajya Sabha was unusually full of foreign correspondants.... a phenomena that should have alerted the Government, but it did not. And of course they got the news abroad.

For three months Swamy was kept hidden by RSS faithful in Bombay and Pune. It was a lonely existence; Swamy's only contact was the RSS man who would come once or twice a day with food, and (more important as far as Swamy was concerned) the newspapers, books and family letters and other correspondence. In such isolation Swamy had time to think out his next plan of action. It was not that easy: the entire police force of India was on the hunt for him; and airports particularly were under strict surveillance.

III

What was keeping him in India too, was the fact that Parliament had started proceedings for his expulsion. It was a hurriedly put-up *fait accompli* sort of proceeding, done with the intention of seeing that Swamy was shorn as urgently as possible, of his Member of Parliament immunities and privileges (I suppose his frequent use (misuse?) of the Rajya Sabha pass must have rankled so there could be no question of waiting patiently, for a further six months' absence to elapse to declare his seat vacant); but it would hardly have been legal without some sort of charge sheet and at least a façade of a hearing.

Normally such a matter as a threatened expulsion of a Member of Parliament would have gone before the Privileges Committee of the Rajya Sabha. But the Privileges Committee had its own laid down procedure and time frame which would have hamstrung the prosecution and slowed it down. So the Government worked out the ingenius, (actually downright disingenuous) scheme of constituting all the members of the Privileges Committee into another Committee with its own easy procedure.

Even then, the procedure was too slow for the taste of the Government. All papers (show cause notice, supporting documents etc.) were sent to our house; and it was then my job to get it across into the RSS pipeline, to Maharashtra wherever Swamy was. There the reply was carefully drafted and signed by Swamy and then returned to me by some equally devious route. And then I had to personally deliver it to the Parliament offices. It speaks volumes of the meticulous organisation of the Sangh, that the process of transmission was never either discovered or derailed by the Police.

The Committee even provided an opportunity for Swamy to appear in person before them; but of course they were denied that treat. Eventually an unanimous Committee pronounced Swamy guilty of the catchall "conduct unbecoming a Member of Parliament" and recommended his expulsion from the Rajya Sabha; and that august body duly expelled him in mid November 1976.

IV

By then, the RSS too was frantic to get Swamy out of India. As Madhav Rao Mule confided to Swamy, Atal Bihari Vajpayee was insisting that Swamy surrender. Apparently Indira Gandhi was adamant on that as a condition for treating with the broken remnants of the Opposition—a group consisting of Vajpayee and two soft Socialists, S. M. Joshi and Nana Gore were proposing to sign some sort of a surrender accepting the need for Indira Gandhi's Twenty Point Programme and legitimacy of the Emergency; but that was being held up because Swamy "was not cooperating".

Madhav Rao Mule was genuinely concerned that if Swamy was imprisoned, a vindictive Indira Gandhi might ensure something terrible was done to his health, (even today it is not clear whether there was not something like that contrived against J.P., who had been perfectly healthy when he was arrested, but had developed an acute kidney problem while incarcerated); so he was keen on getting Swamy out of India safely.

Bhau Rao Deoras, underground brother of the RSS Sarsang Chalak, paid a trip to Kathmandu, to ask for the help of Nepal's King Virendra.

King Virendra had known Swamy when he was a student

at Harvard where Swamy was then teaching, and he had a warm admiration for him, and King Virendra too had a deep respect for the RSS; but, he explained to Bhau Rao that his little kingdom and he too were helpless in the grip of Indira Gandhi if she chose to be vindictive: so he dared not agree to Bhau Rao's first suggestion, that Swamy be shipped out of Delhi in a Royal Nepal Airlines Cargo plane. However King Virendra promised that if Swamy could manage to get to Nepal, he would try to ensure that he was flown abroad from Kathmandu.

So that was what Swamy aimed for. The plan turned out to be quite simple. He was driven from Pune and Bombay through Maharashtra and M.P. and U.P. to Bhairwa on the India-Nepal border. He stopped for a short halt in Lucknow, to meet Vajpayee's emissary Rajju Bhaiya, (years later Rajju Bhaiya became Sar Sang Chalak and was instrumental in destroying Swamy's RSS links), who was openly hostile and demanded that Swamy surrender otherwise the Government might be even more ruthless with the RSS; but of course Swamy was in no mood to heed such advice, since to him it was becoming increasingly clear that an inimical Vajpayee, by now burning with jealousy of Swamy's hero status with the RSS, was quite capable of selling Swamy down the river.

At Bhairwa on the UP-Nepal border, it was known that customs inspection came to a halt some ten minutes before the Post closed for the night at 9 p.m. In that crucial ten minute slot, Swamy walked across the border and got into a rickshaw that was waiting for him in Nepal, and he was driven to the neighbouring airport where King

Virendra had arranged for a plane which flew him to Kathmandu. There was a short halt in Kathmandu, where Swamy was able to meet both King Virendra and his Prime Minister Shri Tulsi Giri as well as some RSS fugitives who had taken refuge in Nepal. Among them was Kedarnath Sahni, former Mayor of Delhi. Kedarnathji was by now fed up being cooped up in Kathmandu and jumped at the chance to move on with Swamy. They both caught a Royal Nepal Airline plane to Bangkok, where they parted company; and Swamy caught a Thai Airline flight to London via Rome.

Even that was not uneventful. The Thai Airline plane developed engine trouble in Rome; and so there were numerous passengers offloaded and looking for alternate rides to London. Swamy, unsure about the consequences if he approached an airline official and that person found he was on a proscribed Indian passport, did not dare demand an alternate ride. Just then almost miraculously, an Italian lady came upto him and asked if he had an Indian passport and whether he had no luggage. When he confirmed both facts, she quietly led him to a London bound plane which was already loaded and ready to leave, and settled him in the sole unfilled first class seat, (Swamy only had an economy ticket). To this day Swamy does not know who and why his benefactress was; but it did save him from possible detention.

V

By December 1976, Swamy was back in Cambridge Massachusetts where loyal friends and colleagues tried to get him resettled in at Harvard. His friend Dean Henry Rosovsky even fought the Harvard Faculty lions and got them to offer Swamy a position in the Economics Department.

Not for long: as Swamy put it dramatically, "There I was in Littauer, (the building housing the Economics Department) in my old chamber ruefully contemplating the seven years since my last position here, when the telephone rang. It was a news agency telling me that back in India, Indira Gandhi had got the Lok Sabha dissolved and fresh General Elections were scheduled for March."

I don't know how many people actually believed that these were going to be genuine elections, free and fair: I know I told Swamy not to come back: he would only be arrested and incarcerated along with all the lakhs already in jail. But Swamy was adamant. When he told Rosovsky that he was giving up his Harvard appointment and returning to India to participate in the elections, Rosovsky was appalled: it had been a tough job persuading Harvard to create at short notice an opening for Swamy; and now Swamy was preparing to throw that away. However when he saw that Swamy was determined, he relented. He agreed but he added a condition. "If your people come to power in India, I will expect you to work for Indian recognition of Israel." Swamy promised; and it was a promise he was able to keep: the next few years under Morarjibhai's prime ministership saw the beginning of a thaw in Indo-Israeli relations; and finally in 1991, when it looked as if the first Israeli Embassy in Delhi would not be able to open its doors on the scheduled date and deadline, Swamy (then a

Union Cabinet Minister) offered his own home for the Embassy to function from for the crucial deadline. So in fact the first visa issued by Israel in Delhi was stamped in our own home.

Chapter XII

THE SECOND YEAR OF THE EMERGENCY

I

While all this was going on viz-a-viz Swamy, at home Swamy's family was reaping the effects of his vanishing act. On the very day of Swamy's Rajya Sabha escapade, by the time I reached home, (I had collected the car and visited my sister en route) the Police had raided my home and temporarily dealt with the cook by locking her into the kitchen, (I can still recall the loud thumps and yells from the kitchen relayed over the phone lines when I phoned up my home from Coomi's house). The drawing room where I was seated by them was awash with police officers who drew out from me a blow by blow account of Swamy's antics. Apparently they were in a puzzle as to how to declare them illegal: one rather admiring officer compared the whole operation to moving one's hand very fast through a candle flame: if this is done really fast there is no injury. While they were attempting to cross examine me, to their further bewilderment, Swamy's cable from Mathura "Book published", was delivered. And I saw no harm in explaining its significance. Apparently the Police promptly sent someone to the Mathura station to try and nab Swamy; but of course the bird had flown away by then.

The only other occupant of our house Satish Singh was discovered by the Police to have quietly left the house just after Swamy left for Parliament; and the Police were not even quite sure whether he actually existed as a separate person or was merely another avatar of Swamy. They followed his trail anyway, and Satish led them a merry dance, muddying the hunt-for-Swamy trail by going off to visit his brother-in-law at a remote inaccessible tea plantation in Assam. When the Police finally caught up with him, it was only to have Satish's brother-in-law vouch for the fact that he was definitely NOT Subramanian Swamy.

At one point the interrogation in my drawing room was interrupted by the arrival of Chu discharged from her nursery school. I shall never forget the pindrop silence as small footsteps were heard hopping up the driveway, with a small voice joyously carolling "Hullo Amma! Hullo Amma! Hullo Amma!" The drawing door was opened, a small figure took one startled look at the assembly, and fled to its bedroom. My sister-in-law and I spent the rest of the day at the Hauz Khas Police Station; tedious but not particularly inquisatorial: no one seemed to know what to do with us.

At another point I phoned home from the Police Station, to find Gitanjali in floods of tears: I had forgotten that she was due at the birthday party next door. My response, "But darling, all you have to do is get dressed and get dropped off by the ayah", showed how little I understood a child's priorities: "But Amma, I have no present to take."…..Finally

Gitanjali solved her own social problems: she went without a present to the Party and when a small tormentor questioned her gift-less arrival, she haughtily demanded, "Am I invited to the Party or is it my present that's invited?"

The next morning, I woke to find that our house was completely surrounded by the police. The ayah found them obstructing her way when she set off to escort Gitanjali to the school bus stop. And Gitanjali, who till then had looked forward greedily to any excuse for a holiday, suddenly started wailing that she wanted to go to school.

I asked the havaldar at the gate as to what the problem was. To my surprise, he picked up his gun, pointed it at my head and pronounced solemnly in Hindi that henceforth, no-one would be allowed out of the house. His words made no impression on me but his action did. With decades of my father's upbringing behind me, I shouted at him, "Put that gun down, you fool. Don't you realise it might be loaded and might go off!"

The poor man was flabbergasted: people with guns pointed at their heads are supposed to cringe and weep. Instead I went on to crisply demand his officer's phone number so I could complain.

Of course, the officer turned out to be a more polished type and after he received my flood of complaints, laced with whatever I had learnt about my rights under the Constitution of India, he agreed that of course Gitanjali could go to school. But that was his only concession.

In some ways poor Gitanjali had the toughest time during the Emergency. In school, she was a marked child: so very few of her classmates were even willing to talk to her. As she later confided to me, she simply quietly worked her way through the school day and returned home sometimes with no interaction with any other child. With almost the only exception of an extremely supportive principal, who never let Swamy's outlaw status stand in the way of her care for Gitanjali, the teachers were as bad as the classmates: some of them did not even hesitate to ask Gitanjali intrusive questions about where her father was and what he was doing.

Some months later, when I felt matters were going beyond the endurance of a mere seven year old, I thought of sending Gitanjali to my brother's family in Canada. So I set about applying to renew her (Indian) passport. To my amazement the reply from the Home Ministry came back: the Government was denying Gitanjali a passport, "in the public interest". After some thought I recollected that one of my fellow students at Harvard had been Rama Mehta, whose husband was in the Foreign Service. Though patently terrified by my presence on her doorstep, Rama was courteous; but she could not help. Another Harvard contact I approached, an IAS officer whose husband was also in the I.A.S., was not even courteous, as the couple hustled me and Sushila out of their home. Obviously the bureaucracy had been terrorised by the Emergency measures.

Because of my Law College course, I knew something about fundamental rights; so I toyed with the idea of filing a Writ Petition on behalf of Gitanjali. I got to work on it, but by then the Emergency was over, and the Petition proved unnecessary: but Government procedures and sensitivities had not undergone any sea-change—as demonstrated when the new government denied a passport to the ex-Prime Minister's daughter-in-law Maneka Gandhi. Unlike Gitanjali, Maneka was an adult; and there might even have been a scintilla of "public interest" in denying her a passport; but in a land mark judgement Maneka Gandhi VS. Union of India, seven judges of the Supreme Court upheld her fundamental right to travel abroad as well as her right to a hearing and a reasoned denial. Of course I applaud the judgment; but it would have been some small self-satisfaction if before it was filed the matter had been already decided by the courts in a Writ Petition, In the Matter of Gitanjali Swamy Through Her Mother and Natural Guardian Vs. Union of India.

But the cream of the passport fracas did not come to my knowledge until some forty years later in the month of July in this Year of Grace 2016. During the Emergency I had never applied for a passport for our second daughter Suhasini (Chu), aged about three years old; but after my application on behalf of Gitanjali had been received and rejected, the powers that be felt they must take precautions against any wicked attempt on my part to get a passport for Chu. Apparently on 2.2.1977, at the tail end of the Emergency, the Regional Passport Office, Delhi, was issued an instruction F7(3)/77-Pol I(D/11269/77) stating:

"SUHASINI SHERENE SWAMY
d/o (PROF) SUBRAMANIAN SWAMY
Born DELHI 19/2/73
RESIDENT N 226 GREATER KAILASH I, NEW DELHI
PRO Delhi req: Passport should NOT be granted without prior reference to R.P.O. Delhi."

That instruction continues unrescinded till today. In July this year Chu, now the respectable forty year old Diplomatic Affairs Editor of the national daily "Hindu", with a father-in-law who had once actually headed the Ministry of External Affairs itself, appeared for the follow up on her routine application for fresh pages for her current passport. She was confronted by a rooky passport issuing clerk with apparently no knowledge of either Chu's lineage or her subsequent antecedents, who explained that because of the 1977 ukase she could do nothing but refer the matter to the higher-ups for instructions. It took Chu the rest of the day to get the fresh passport pages she had applied for. (Apparently when he heard about the fracas, the Secretary MEA told Chu who was quite friendly with him that the Lookout Notice of 1977, demonstrated how prescient the MEA was: they had already figured out in 1977 that the three year old Chu might be a menace to society). With the Media's present attitude towards Subramanian Swamy, Chu would have been assured front page banner headlines if she had chosen to air her grievance; but rather to my disappointment she did not.

II

Anyway, passport fracas aside, there followed days and months of the Police sleuthing us. I continued my Law School classes, acutely aware that the Police were always there at the back of the class. But even there, there were ways of evading them: I remember meeting a Vidyarthi Parishad volunteer in the Library stacks where he would hand over letters from Swamy, which might have gone through half a dozen hands before reaching me. I remember how cheerful they always were. Once I picked up the telephone to be greeted by a fake squeaky Heathen Chinese greeting, "This is Mr. Moto Moto speaking."... Nothing ever keeps Swamy down, not even the fact that the mythical Mr. Moto Moto would have to be Japanese and not Chinese.

On one of those days my brother-in-law Dr. K.S. Srikantan arrived in Delhi, (he was working for the U.N. in New York) for a population conference. Sushila told him over the phone that he could not stay with us because of the Police surveillance; so Srikantan went across to my brother-in-law's Bengali Market flat. He was fast asleep there when he was woken up by a flurry of urgent knocks. The Police had traced him and demanded that he open up in the name of the law, as they had a warrant for his arrest.

Srikantan is nothing if not cool and rational. He retorted that if they had such a warrant, they should slip it under the door so he could study it. There was a stunned silence. Apparently no one had ever asked these police men to actually see their warrant. After some confabulation, the Police produced an officer who through the door informed Srikantan that he was senior enough and could arrest without a warrant. So Srikantan let him in.

The Officer then told Srikantan, "Dr. Swamy, you are under arrest."

Srikantan replied, "But I am not Swamy. My name is Srikantan. And Swamy is my brother-in-law"

Officer, "Can you prove that?."

Srikantan, "Well here is my passport and my invitation to the Population Conference."

Officer," At least you will admit you are a Tamilian and you look like Dr. Swamy."

Srikantan, "You know, my dear sir, not all Tamilians look alike. In fact obviously Swamy's face is definitely dolichocephallic and my face is unmistakably brachicephallic. Your people's investigation is quite unscientific."

At that point the poor Officer grasped two handfuls of his hair and told Srikantan, "Dr. Srikantan, since your brother-in-law returned, I have not had a moments' peace."

Chapter XIII

SWAMY IS EXPELLED FROM THE RAJYA SABHA

I

Quite a lot of other people must have been in the same boat. Parliament, which had counted on unseating Swamy by the simple expedient that he had stayed absent from Parliament for a continuous period of sixty days, (there is such a constitutional provision), found it would have to take the tough route of actually expelling him—a rather grey area, made even murkier by the fact that they did not have either a genuine case of illegal behaviour or even moral turpitude on which to pin the expulsion, nor did they want to follow the laid out procedure.

Besides Swamy was not even cooperating by turning up for the hearings (he was still absconding). In his defence I might point out that he did offer to appear before the House provided he was assured safe conduct—a demand the House haughtily disregarded and refused to reply to. So in the end the Committee (a parallel Committee with the same membership but not the official designation of Privileges Committee) simply recommended Swamy's expulsion for "conduct unbecoming a Member of Parliament".

The actual format of the Committee's finding against him read as follows:

> "The Committee finds Mr. Swamy's conduct as derogatory of the House, its members and inconsistent with the standards which the House is entitled to expect of its members.
>
> There is no doubt that Mr. Subramanian Swamy had deliberately violated the law by travelling on a passport which he knew was impounded. He also did not appear before this Committee in spite of repeated directions in that behalf. His description of Parliament as our captive Parliament and the innuendos he has made against the members show his utter disrespect to the parliamentary institutions of the country and amount to contempt of the House and its members."

So in November 1976, Swamy earned another first: he was the first M.P. to be expelled from the Rajya Sabha.

II

Swamy's expulsion, also showed me how small, mean, envious and malicious a man was Atal Bihari Vajpayee, the Parliamentary Leader of the Jan Sangh.

After Swamy's expulsion, we set about challenging the expulsion in the Courts. Naturally I expected the support of Swamy's political party the Jan Sangh; so I went to their advocate our friend Appa Ghatate. But Appa told me he had instructions not to touch the case; and that I should talk directly to Vajpayee about it. So I did so.

I found Vajpayee at his home on Ferozshah Road. Sleek and at his ease in all the comfort of these surroundings, he was being looked after by the family of his foster daughter. I told him how shocked I was by his refusal to support Swamy, who had sacrificed so much including his family life and security. Vajpayee was defiant. He expressed himself angered by Swamy's "wrong doings" which he said, was damaging the credibility of the Jan Sangh.

What exactly was this wrongdoing as Vajpayee saw it?: Swamy had signed for and collected some Rs. 400 or Rs.500 daily allowance by "claiming" to have attended Parliament on the days immediately before and after Parliament met in June 1975. I pointed out that it was I who had filled in the proforma application which had been signed by Swamy; and that it very clearly claimed the money because Swamy had travelled to Delhi "with the intention of attending Parliament", all of which was what the law required, (apparently the law did not require actual attendance in Parliament, only to have the intention to so attend)and all of which was true. Vajpayee instead kept insisting piously that this amount was the "fruit of corruption", and so the Jan Sangh's good name would be spoilt if it supported Swamy in his challenge to his expulsion: "The amount may be small; but it is corruption", he stated piously.

I was deeply hurt; but it soon became clear to me that this was only a catspaw: internally Vajpayee was seething because anyone could see the contrast between Swamy's heroic and selfless struggle for which he had sacrificed his family's wellbeing and comfort and Vajpayee's self indulgence in the arms of the family of his foster daughter. I left in disgust. It was the last time I ever spoke to Vajpayee. After the Emergency he tried to meet me; but I have always ignored him. I do not regret it in the least. The man has known all along that Swamy is the better man; and he has done all he can to victimise him and keep him out. If I have never completely reconciled with the RSS, it is because in all those years, even though they knew Swamy was blameless, policy dictated that their future development required that they fall in line with Vajpayee. For years they kept Swamy cut off from his natural allies. That Swamy survived and flourished despite this, shows how resilient and unshakable he is.

Finally, when you consider the literally hundreds of crores that Vajpayee, his foster daughter's family and his friends and creatures are reputed to have made while in power, I find it laughable that he could have castigated Swamy for his "corruption" of a few hundred rupees.

III

I have nothing but contempt for the manner in which Vajpayee reacted to Swamy; but by now, after Swamy has been in public life for nearly half a century, I am convinced that at least in India, this trait is very frequently found among the insecure and second rate among politicians. As long as an "aspirant" "knows his place" and does not do anything to threaten another politician's ascendancy, he will be tolerated, even advanced. But the slightest independent advancement—even if it is for the common goal—brings out the meanest streak in the insecure second rater; and then everything must be done to crush the supposed emerging rival. Why single out Vajpayee, when his behaviour is the norm among so many!

Another aspect of the same insecurity is that when some person actually encourages and advances his juniors, these same junior beneficiaries consider him as a fool and have no sense of gratitude for such generosity. On the contrary, they attempt to build themselves up by spreading nasty stories about their fellow Ministers, through their sidekicks in the Press.

In Swamy's life, he has seen and benefitted by both kinds of experiences; by the generosity and encouragement of great men like his thesis advisor Simon Kusnets and his other mentor Paul Samuelson, like his dear friends and promoters in the Jan Sangh Nanaji Deshmukh and Dattopant Thengadi, and even by a comparative outsider like Morajibhai Desai; and he has experienced in great measure the dog–eat-dog wolf-pack mentality of persons like Atal Bihari Vajpayee and his side-kicks. It has left him imbued with a nobler but more detached philosophy as enshrined in the Bhagavad Gita: you have only the obligation to act to do your duty, no right to or expectation of the fruits of such action.

Anyway, without any assistance from the Jan Sangh, Swamy prepared the papers of his challenge to his expulsion through the eminent jurist Mr. M.C. Chagla, whose selfless work thereon we shall always remember with deep gratitude.

Chapter XIV

THE 1977 ELECTIONS

It proved to be unnecessary. Elections were declared in January of the following year; Swamy fought and won a Lok Sabha Seat from Maharashtra; and never regretted the loss of the earlier Rajya Sabha seat.

It was a triumphal passage. When Swamy landed from the U.S. in Bombay, before cheering crowds, the RSS decided that he would get a much better reception and reaction, if instead of catching a flight to Delhi, he took the train. Huge and delirious crowds gathered to cheer and garland him at Bombay Central Station, and at all the train stops between Bombay and Delhi; and the final reception at the New Delhi station was spectacular. I took the children with me to receive him there; and the crowds were so large and enthusiastic that even we were practically swept away; and a frantic Chu wept and wept because she lost her slippers in the melee.

After that Swamy had a few days in Delhi while it was decided where he would stand from in the ensuing elections; and I wanted him to use that time to clean up his act. He was after all, still a wanted absconder; and at sometime in those years of absconding, I had appeared before the concerned Magistrate and undertaken that Swamy would appear before him as soon as he was back in India. Swamy was reluctant to honour my promise, (he really did not know how Authority would react to such a surrender and whether he would not simply be whisked off to Tihar Jail); but I was persistent, and he went to the Police Court, (where I believe instructions had indeed been passed to arrest him). He was saved from an ignominious arrest simply because the Court was not sitting that day: the President Fakhruddin Ali Ahmad had passed away and all courts were closed in mourning. Till today Swamy has never let me forget that bad advice I gave him, when only providence saved him from an arrest and incarceration, which might well have put him out of the running for the Lok Sabha that year since he would not have been able to file his nomination papers as required.

As it was, Vajpayee even tried to block Swamy's claims to a Lok Sabha seat. Vajpayee had been cultivating the Lucknow constituency, (you may recall Swamy had worked there in 1973 to 1975), but this was eventually snaffled by H.N. Bahuguna; so Vajpayee stood from the New Delhi seat, which should have gone to Swamy, who as President of the New Delhi Jan Sangh, had nurtured that seat for several years. The only other seat Swamy had some sort of a claim to, South Madras, was given to Acharya Kripalani, because the wily Karunanidhi did not want Swamy around his territory. In fact almost all the tickets to likely seats for Swamy had been given out to other claimants when finally the RSS took a hand; and it was decided to put Swamy up from Bombay North East, (a seat that had always sent a Congress M.P.), to which Swamy really had the thinnest of claims (actually my family was based in South Bombay and it was only much later after the elections were over, that it emerged that our family's lands were three villages in the Bombay North East constituency).

In the Congress debacle of 1977, it did not matter where a Janata Party candidate stood from; and Swamy won handily from the then largest constituency in India, Bombay North East, which till that year he had never even visited. I have participated in elections and election victories since; but never again have I experienced the public euphoria of those days. It culminated in a huge illuminated truck victory procession which wound its way from Chembur to Ghatkopar to Mulund, which everyone else enjoyed actually dancing inside the trucks and on the roads outside while I stood petrified in the truck, terrified that one or other of the illuminating electric torches making threatening sizzling noises would blow us all up. I remember little Chu was with friends in quite another truck; and Gitanjali later went around proclaiming to all and sundry that poor Chu had gone by mistake in a Congress truck. Totally false: no Congress truck was out on the streets of Bombay on that day.

Chapter XV

THE JANATA PARTY GOVERNMENT YEARS

I

Well, after that, family life went back to normal; but it was long before the children finally forgot those Emergency days, and their hatred of the Congress name. Once I remember Chu burst into tears because in a fit of spite, Gitanjali gave her the ultimate insult of calling her "Chu Chu Gandhi" (Swamy smacked her for this). Another time, when Swamy, the kids and I went walking at night in New Delhi, the kids lagging behind, I turned to hear delighted giggles: the children were amusing themselves adding Dracula teeth, long ears and snakes to the remaining Indira Gandhi election posters that still hung around. Finally one day when we took the kids to Parliament and gave them lunch there, in a rather crowded dining room, we offered a seat at our table to the Leader of the Opposition, the much respected C.M. Stephen. Half way through the meal, Gitanjali dragged Swamy out, to confidentially warn him that he did not seem to realise that the kindly uncle sitting at our table was actually a Congress monster.

I had entered the Parliamentary environs with not much knowledge of how a Member's family conducts itself; but I did have some vague idea that we must conduct our lives with "Gandhian" simplicity. So for our first trip back to Bombay, I booked the whole family into an ordinary second class compartment. Swamy had left the arrangement entirely to me; and it was only when he arrived at the station that he was outraged to realise that he was not to be housed in the large airconditioned compartment of his tastes. He waited only till the first station Faridabad, to get us all transferred to the air conditioned coach he was entitled to, leaving me with a flea in my ear. He was not, he said, a hypocritical Gandhian and he had every intention of continuing to live in the comfort he was entitled to. He has continued in that mould: hardly any family I know has as many air conditioners and TVs and computers as we do—as you could expect, most of them just dropped into Swamy's extended hand; and the worst is that most of them are switched on for most of the time. Unlike the situation amongst us Parsis, the size of his electricity bill has never been a matter of interest or concern for Swamy.

However, I did learn then that the days of Gandhian simplicity among politicians are long past. As to privileges like mere out-of-turn allotments of seats in railway trains, the M.P. of the post Freedom Struggle days, thinks these are his as a matter of right. People with a Parsi background, enhanced by the Maharashtrian middleclass disciplines of a schooling in Bombay, have standing in queues and waiting their turn, ingrained in their blood; so it came as a surprise that the rest of the privileged political classes do not. Two early instances come very much to my mind. One summer in Bangalore I found to my dismay that our family's return train tickets to Delhi were not confirmed. I phoned up Swamy for help and he fixed up that I should go and see the Chief Minister Shri Gundu Rao. Gundu Raoji was all kindness and courtesy, and he obliged; but I could see that he was genuinely puzzled that a VIP's wife could want nothing more of him than a mere ticket confirmation. So as a small bonus he insisted we share a truly splendid breakfast with him. On another occasion I found that the Minister for Railways, Mr. Ghani Khan Chaudary had even more lavish ideas: faced with my humble request for three confirmed sleeper berths Bombay-Delhi, to my embarrassment, he had a whole extra bogey laid on.

Delhi citizens of those years, unlike their Bombay counterparts, had no idea what a queue is. (I suspect they still do not). As a rather elderly law school student, during and after the Emergency I can remember overawing fashionable young sprigs from the better known Delhi colleges: convinced of their own inalienable right to out-of-turn bus seat allotment, they had worked out a system: one young twerp would roll up early to the waiting buses and walk along the bus corridor putting a book down on each seat: thereafter the "booked" seats were appropriated as of right by his late-coming cronies. Of course, young girl students of that generation were too shy to protest. ("Ma'am, if we made a fuss, we would get noticed and our parents would be so ashamed of us!"). Not so Dr. (Mrs.) Subramanian Swamy who made all these boys get up, remove those books and stand in queues. The Bombay habit is too deeply ingrained; I am still in the habit of making customers in my bank and people in the shops queue up—much to Swamy's amusement, nay embarrassment.

II

Vajpayee's jealousy and malice followed Swamy over all the following years. Morarjibhai's cabinet was on a quota basis: each of the parties which had joined together to form the Janata Party decided its own nominees, and Vajpayee saw to it that Swamy got nothing from the Jan Sangh quota. To keep him from being included in the Government, he insisted that Swamy was needed for Party work; but then he saw to it that Swamy was not included in the Party's National Executive. However his open hostility at every turn had one interested spectator: the Prime Minister, who in a quiet way made a friend of, guide to and confidante of Swamy. Thus Morarjibhai saw to it that Swamy was made a member of the Janata Party Parliamentary Board (it was an election in which Morarjibhai and Nanaji Deshmukh joined to ensure that Swamy won even while a far more senior man, L.K. Advani lost): from which post we family members got an unusual bonus. On Independence Day, when the Prime Minister made his annual speech to the Nation, from the ramparts of Red Fort, Swamy not only got to sit there on the ramparts, but he actually managed to get his family there. I don't think Gitanjali aged 8 and Chu aged 4 realised what an unique privilege they had; but certainly I shall never forget it: to sit up there on the heights and see the delirious populace (it was still glowing from the election results) and Chandni Chowk stretching out below us.

As a member of the Parliamentary Board, Swamy was invited to various key meetings. He was also made the President of the Yuva Janata, in which were inducted all the enthusiastic young men who had belonged to the RSS and been inducted in the Janata Party. Years later, even after decades of subsequent blackballing of Swamy by the BJP, these young men, who had by then risen to the front ranks of the BJP, could be relied on to unobtrusively support Swamy at crucial times.

One very interesting sidelight of those days of which Swamy strongly approved was one small word missing in the Janata Party Constitution. The Socialists naturally wanted to include a declaration that the Janata Party believed in Gandhian Socialism; but fortunately there were at least two ancient stalwarts of the Freedom Struggle who were adamantly opposed: Morarjibhai (with the common sense conservatism that is almost a hallmark of being Gujarati) and Chaudhary Charan Singh (the latter you may recall, had managed to foil Jawaharlal Nehru's Plan for the collectivisation of Indian agriculture); and eventually it was merely laid down that the Janata Party stood for a Gandhian Way of Life.

Interestingly, despite the later long years of dissension within the Janata Party, till the end it kept that declaration. The surprising thing was that later when the conservative and right-wing Bharatiya Janata Party (the BJP) was formed from the former RSS elements in the Janata Party, it was

Vajpayee with his determination to polish his image among the more respectable, more "progressive" members of society, who insisted on the BJP being declared a believer in Gandhian Socialism.

III

Swamy's activities in and around the first Janata regime, too upset Vajpayee. He was the External Affairs Minister and one area he wanted to shine in was as the developer of friendly relations between India and China. Unfortunately for his ambitions, this was an area in which Swamy had already established himself. In the early seventies, when Sino-Indian relations were still frozen in the aftermath of the 1962 Sino-Indian War and when no-one of note would have thought of so much as stepping inside the Chinese Embassy, Swamy had made a practice of visiting there and showing his interest in their concerns. I can remember outings in the early nineteen seventies when as we drove into the Chinese Embassy grounds, Indian Intelligence heads would poke out of the bushes outside the grounds to note who had had the temerity to enter the largely shunned Chinese Embassy; but the Chinese staff was delighted to see a friendly Indian face. It helped that Swamy actually spoke Mandarin: he had studied it at Harvard where a rigorous drilling had ensured that he spoke it with an impeccably correct accent often viewed with awe by the native Chinese speakers, (many of whom spoke Mandarin with the heavy vernacular accent of their native provinces). So it was not at all surprising that when the Janata Party Government was formed in 1977, his old acquaintances in the Chinese Embassy came to him with an invitation that we visit China. Vajpayee objected: he had set his heart on being the first notable Indian to be received in China. But Morarjibhai insisted that Swamy go first; and he saw to it too that Swamy received every facility and backup from our Embassy there.

Interestingly our ambassador in China was K.R. Narayanan, who later became President of India under a Congress dispensation. In the late sixties when Swamy was teaching at Harvard and making a comparative study of the economies of India and China, he had called on Narayanan then an officer in Delhi in the Ministry of External Affairs, to try and get a Chinese entry on his Indian Passport, (in those days Indian passports invariably contained a statement that such passport was not valid for entry to Israel, South Africa and China). Narayanan curtly refused his request, stating that, "No patriotic Indian would want to visit China at all". Now, as ambassador, it was his rather painful duty to facilitate and backup Swamy's interaction with our Chinese hosts. His attempts at friendship were not shared by his spouse, a haughty Burmese lady who when she found that I was a teetotaller, gave me a lecture on how it was my duty as an Indian abroad to maintain cordial relations with the natives by drinking liquor with them. Needless to say I was as haughty and obdurate in my views as she was in hers'.

Our Chinese hosts took very seriously Swamy's interest in developing friendly relations, (indeed any relations at all) between India and China. One thing Swamy suggested was that there be reopened the age old Hindu pilgrim route through the Himalayas and onto the Tibetan plateau, to Kailash and Manasarovar, (which route had been closed since the 1962 War). To Beijing several thousand miles east of these holy places of an unfamiliar faith, these were quite new ideas. I remember one official visited us in our Beijing hotel rooms, to ask Swamy to write down the names of these places of pilgrimage; and between us, Swamy and I debated just how Manasarovar should be spelt and indeed how pronounced!! ...but the germ of the suggestion was mulled over by the Chinese. Some years later, when Swamy on another trip, was granted a meeting with the then restored Chinese strongman Deng Tsaio Ping, Deng told him that it had been decided to reopen the old pilgrim route. A few months thereafter, the Chinese ambassador came to call on Swamy with the news that the reopening had been worked out with the Indian Government, that the first batch of twenty pilgrims were to be allowed that summer; and, he added, of course Swamy must be in that first batch.

I was rather amused. We had just come back from a family holiday in Bhim Tal where the Gangotri Yatra had been advertised; and I had suggested to Swamy that it might be fun to trek there, a matter of two or three days; and Swamy had retorted, "Do you think I am mad enough to go trekking through the mountains for so many days!"... now here was a trip that would take not four days but four weeks—a fortnight going and a fortnight returning on a mule track at dizzy heights, entering the Tibetan plateau through the Lipu Lekh Pass at nearly 18,000 feet. And of course, Swamy could not refuse.

Well, Swamy could not refuse; but he did manoeuvre himself a less onerous route. By then Indira Gandhi was once more Prime Minister; and surprisingly, Swamy and she had worked out a rather friendly if guarded relationship. (At her request, Swamy had persuaded the Chinese to disown Arunachal rebels who had entered China and looked to China for succour; and the Chinese had obliged). So Swamy asked her whether for the return journey, she could arrange for an Indian Air Force helicopter to pick him up below Lipu Lekh, and fly him over the mountains to the Air Force Station at Bareilly. Apparently she first teased him by suggesting that it would suit her more if a troublesome person like Swamy went to Tibet and never returned; but then she laughed and promised that she would get it done. So while his journey into Tibet was an onerous two weeks of trudging in the mountains, then a jeep ride across the flat Tibetan plateau and a quick view of the truly spectacular Mount Kailash, of the legendary Manasarovar Lake and of Lake Rakshashsthal, (where Ravana had earned his powers by doing penance), on his return journey Swamy separated from his fellow travellers and got the Chinese escort to drive him upto Lipu Lekh. He crossed the Pass on foot and there immediately below the Pass he was relieved to find the Indian Air Force helicopter awaiting his arrival. In a few hours he was in Bareilly and in yet another few hours he was in an Air Force plane and heading to Delhi. So he arrived back in Delhi a good two weeks ahead of the other pilgrims.

IV

But here, (the pilgrimage took place in 1981) I am going a good few years ahead of Swamy's first trip to China in September 1978. Nothing if not controversial, Swamy suggested there that the troubled border issue might be solved by working out a "mutually maintainable" boundary line, made without reference to the actual line on the ground that patriotic Indians were supposed to swear by. The suggestion was received with angry protests in India; and we returned to be greeted by a full scale demonstration against us organised by Raj Narain and his followers. I have always suspected that Vajpayee, then External Affairs Minister and nursing a grievance that with Morarjibhai's concurrence, Swamy had managed to steal a march on him by getting to China first, was also instrumental behind the demonstration because at the airport we were met by my relative, an ardent follower of Vajpayee, who shouted at and castigated Swamy as a "traitor" in suggesting an agreement with China—a view that Vajpayee assiduously spread.

Vajpayee's own China visit, in February 1979, turned out to be a disaster. The Chinese have long memories. They remembered that the 1960's Indo-Soviet Friendship Treaty, (under which both the parties undertook to support each other in case of a war between either of them and China) had been passed by the Indian Parliament with the support of the then Jan Sangh led by Vajpayee. They also remembered with gratitude that Morarjibhai had been opposed to the Treaty and also that as Prime Minister, when it looked as if China and Russia would come to blows over conflicting claims on the Ussuri River Islands, Morarjibhai had bluntly told the Russians that despite the obligations of the Treaty, India would not allow Russian troops to enter Tibet through India. So the Chinese set about humiliating Vajpayee during his trip. His airplane was made to develop some trouble or other and the Chinese expressed themselves quite unable to quickly produce a replacement, so Vajpayee was kept hanging around for some days in his hotel room. Worse still, while he was still in China, an armed conflict arose between China and North Vietnam (if he had not been so fixated on effecting an early Chinese visit, Vajpayee, would have seen that conflict coming, and not gone at all); and Vajpayee had to cut his visit to China short; so he had nothing to show for his trip.

Chapter XVI

THE BREAK WITH THE RSS AND JAN SANGHIS

I

All the above must have been yet another thorn in Vajpayee's side; and it was a grievance nursed at low boil until openly revealed in 1980, when the former Jan Sangh members split away from the Janata Party and formed a rival party the Bharatiya Janata Party (the BJP). Vajpayee was of course the unchallenged leader of the BJP; and he made it clear that he would not tolerate the presence of Swamy in the BJP. The RSS fell in line with Vajpayee with the result that Swamy, who had great faith in the RSS steadfastness, was let down. A fellow Member of Parliament Shri Yagya Dutt Sharma was sent to tell Swamy that they did not want Swamy in their new party and that if he wished to retain any goodwill in the BJP, he should be prepared for a long "van vas" in the boon docks.

"Van vas", by the way is a truly evocative Sanskrit phrase referring to the fourteen year exile that Shri Ramachandraji undertook. The same "van vas" was offered to at least two other persons, close friends of Swamy, whom the jealous

Vajpayee regarded as possible rivals: Nanaji Deshmukh (the organisor par excellence of the Jan Sangh and its powerful treasurer and liason with the business world) and Dattopant Thengadi, (who had selflessly developed the Jan Sangh's labour wing the Bharatiya Majdoor Sangh). Nanaji and Dattopantji, two disciplined RSS workers since their boyhood, fell in line and left Delhi to work selflessly in the mofussil. Swamy, who had no such constraints, continued defiant in the Janata Party.

The real sufferer was me who discovered that most of our RSS friends and their families with whom we had developed friendships over the years of togetherness, simply walked out on us. To understand the extent of the loss one has to know and experience, (as we had done throughout the 1970s) the intimate ties and warm hospitality within Jan Sangh families. India is huge and to keep in touch with the whole country, in any political party, there is much travel throughout the length and breadth of India; and in the Jan Sangh it was customary to put up visiting Party workers in the homes of local Party supporters. (I am told that this was also the custom in Congress families in the Freedom Struggle days). It was not just that there were less streamlined hotels and guest houses available in those days; or that what was available would have been hard on the Party's small budget; but this was also a wonderful way for likeminded people and families to get to know each other. That Swamy, who had so much to educate Party workers in, (especially because his views gelled with theirs'), should have been made welcome in people's homes, might not have been so surprising. But in those days I travelled a lot with Swamy; and even though it was not so usual for wives to turn up, and even though sometimes the welcoming committee was somewhat puzzled by Swamy's short tressed companion who did not wear bangles and a bindi, I was always welcomed and made to feel part of the family. Whether it was Ujjain or Surat or Dharwad or Lucknow or Chandigarh or Bhavnagar or even Madras, it was so heart warming to be welcomed and looked after in people's homes and to mingle with their wives, children and grandchildren. One might think that I, with my rather anglicised ways and rather stilted Hindi and very little experience of the concerns and traditions of orthodox Hindu ladies, would have been looked at a little askance by my hostesses. But it was not so: I made friends with these families and would meet them again and again wherever the Jan Sangh had its sessions, and exchange notes on children and grandchildren. There were also regal families, like Rajmata Scindhia and her children, who had been unfailingly charming, kind and hospitable.

Such bonds were further cemented during the dark Emergency years when I had experienced their caring supervision. For example, I remember with deep affection Chamanlalji, my contact. He was a simple dedicated and sincere Swayam Sevak who before Partition had brought up a whole generation of young lads in the North West Frontier Province and later in Delhi, all of whom remembered him with deep reverence. I do not think he ever became their guru only because he had no intellectual pretensions at all: some of his protegees later rose to high places but they never forgot their initial upbringing by him. In his simple sincere dedicated selfless way, he represented to me the best of the RSS system–I do not believe that the Communist or Maoist cadres, with their cold commissar outlook no matter how dedicated and self sacrificing, can produce great humans like him. He was old by the time the Emergency broke up the RSS Karyalaya that was his home; but he did not hesitate to go out into the cold world; and carry out whatever odd jobs the Organisors wanted of him. He would stand for hours at some designated corner waiting to deliver a letter to or receive a letter from me; or tell me little jokes to keep my spirits up. He was unfailingly caring with no concern for his own comfort or prestige. But he was obedient and disciplined; and I do not think I met him ever again after the break.

III

Suddenly, with Vajpayee's ukase, all this simple warmth with our RSS friends, was cut-off. And so peremptorily and decisively that for instance, when in 1982 Swamy and I went to cast our votes in the MLA Assembly elections in the Bombay North East constituency, (we had intended to vote for the BJP candidate), we discovered that even friends and party workers in Bombay with whom we had stayed for years, and who had always safeguarded our election cards, made all sorts of excuses but would not give us the election cards or even tell us which booths we were registered at. It was almost like being thrown out of a medieval caste set up, with "hookah pani bandh".

Which is why now I am wary of reposing the same

trust and friendship ever again. Swamy has long since reconciled to them; and they, finding him useful and likeminded, are warm and supportive. As for me, appreciative as I continue of their high moral character and ideals which I do share, I am, as I said, wary.

During that period from 1981 onwards, I feel that there has been a terrible tragedy perpetrated on so many of the young idealists who emerged from the RSS school and were absorbed into the BJP cadres. I knew so many of these young persons during and immediately after the Emergency years: youths with nothing much more than an education, a couple of sets of spare clothes on a string clothes line and a "khatiya" in one corner of an RSS karyalaya; and it has pained me to see them metamorphise, under Vajpayee's tutelage and example, into enormously wealthy and powerful individuals, but touts bereft of their earlier moral moorings and often of vicious habits. Perhaps the old Gandhian freedom fighters, seeing the post independence change in the Congress Party, might understand my feelings.

The animosity in the BJP against Swamy continued for a good more than thirty years. Even after Vajpayee was felled by a stroke in 2009, (whereafter he has been a vegetable for all practical purposes), the animosity against Swamy was continued and stoked by Vajpayee's sidekicks; and it was only after herculean efforts by a reconstituted and more just RSS, that Swamy was finally inducted into the BJP in 2013.

Most recently I saw a Vajpayee-like ploy on Swamy slickly and effectively carried out by one such sidekick, now a power in his own right having slithered his way almost to the top of the greasy pole, without benefit of a single contested election win under his belt. In the 2014 general election prelude, it was universally expected that Swamy would be given a ticket to contest; but (as we had discovered in 1977) all the likely tickets were gradually distributed elsewhere. Finally he was promised the BJP Lok Sabha ticket for the New Delhi constituency. The announcement was delayed day after day even though the then President of the Delhi BJP kept personally assuring Swamy that he was the unanimous choice of the New Delhi BJP, that it would be given to him alone and had even urged him to start campaigning in the constituency. Finally on the last night of ticket distribution, the sidekick saw to it that the ticket went elsewhere: on the insulting plea that the nation's capital must be represented only by a Punjabi!: a true pupil of his master.

Such snakes continue to live upto their Vajpayee training in malice and intrigue. They have never cared to cultivate any Party cadres, preferring an excellent raport with the Lutyens Press, the industrialist supporters of the BJP and even an understanding with the Congress. They have risen largely on the heft and goodwill of the BJP supremos, who appear to repose immense confidence in them. I have no cast iron basis for my take on this; but I do have a gut feeling that it is based on a flawed perception that such snakes can deliver the economic goods; and now, more than two years down the line, it is becoming very apparent that no such goods have been or indeed, can be, delivered by an over-promising and not particularly qualified snake.

Besides, if Congress thought that they could maintain a hold on the BJP Government, through such friendly Trojan horses, they must, by now, be pretty disillusioned; and perhaps they will cease to support them from outside.

With the instinct for self preservation, honed by centuries of brahminical skill, (which Vajpayee certainly had developed to perfection) in zeroing in on and cutting out the possibly rising rival, naturally such snakes or their masters appear to have an aversion to giving any rope at all to Swamy. When Swamy had last minute, been denied the New Delhi ticket in 2014, there had been a definite promise ("word of a thakur"), that the very first Rajya Sabha ticket thereafter would be his; but two years down the line, while dozens of people were given BJP tickets and seats, Swamy was not accommodated with anything that he would want to aspire to, (he had made it quite clear that he does not want a Governorship, an Ambassadorship or even a world class banking assignment). The snakes seemed to have adopted the "declare-Swamy-a-political-non-person" technique, that the leftists of the early 1970s had utilised against Swamy. …but the 2010s of this century are not the 1970s of the last; his opponents are nowhere near as powerful or as skilled or as connected as the leftist-Congress-elite combine that dominated, nay ruled, India then; and most important of all, the Swamy of today, is definitely not the naïve, trusting, relatively friendless and unbacked scholar who had returned to India in 1969. Swamy has had to fend for himself outside the BJP organisation; and master and persistent tactician that he is, he has proceeded to develop his own independent formidable organisation, network and dedicated following. So the Rajya Sabha nomination finally given him this year, may well turn out to be the foot in the door.

A warning footnote to this latest Parliament membership is necessary. On 24.6.2016, Harish Khare, editorialising in the Tribune, in an article headed "Carry on Doctor Swamy", had encouraged Swamy to continue in his war on corruption and misgovernance: "You, on the other hand have nothing to fear. You now have six years in the Rajya Sabha", he declared. Apparently Mr. Khare has forgotten about Swamy's first stint in the Rajya Sabha when a six year term was abruptly ended in less than three years on the plea of "conduct unbecoming a member of parliament".

Chapter XVII

SWAMY IN HIS LIGHTER MOMENTS

Swamy has no feel for or curiosity whatsoever about art or literature or cuisine or any other country's proud traditions.

In Paris where his friend Ashok took him as a treat to a world famous restaurant, Swamy had the menu card painstakingly translated for him and then settled for what he thought looked like a promising treat: it turned out to be good old American French fries. Our friend, fellow M.P. Piloo Modi, an amateur chef adept in both Western and Parsi cuisine, once invited Swamy to share some carefully selected sauce savoury he had spent hours slowly simmering; he was outraged when Swamy politely asked for some ketchup to spice it up. But Swamy adores Chinese food and could probably live indefinitely on it.

When I escorted Swamy to colonial Williamsburg or to Washington's Mount Vernon, I found I was viewing them alone while Swamy and Satish Singh sat in the sun and discussed politics in India. He was thrilled with the waterpower of Niagara; but though on the way he obliged me by taking in the Toronto Museum with its superb collection of Chinese porcelain, he took no interest except to try and decipher some of the scrolls: he did not succeed because I think sixteenth century Chinese is different from what he had learnt in the Harvard halls. And of course Swamy loved Disneyland.

The Egyptian government very kindly closed down the public entrance to the Pyramid of Cheops at Giza so that we could enjoy a private tour through its tunnel, but it was wasted on Swamy. It is true he was stunned by the magnificence of the Son-et-Lumiere programme in Luxor; but after that he was just as happy to go back to the hotel and relax over a U.S. cowboy thriller on TV.

In Israel, he was far more interested in talking in his rather broken Marathi to the home-sick Maharashtrian kibutzniks of a Bene Israel kibbutz above the Golan Heights, or marvelling at the extremely productive Israeli cow, (he straight away thought Chaudhary Charan Singh might be interested and wanted the Israelis to send the Chaudhary a sample), than in seeing the thrilling excavations around Jerusalem. But anywhere in the world, he delights in meeting and talking to politicians and scholars.

Incidentally, the Chinese have the almost unique distinction of having forced Swamy to fall in with their idea of what a proper tourist should see of the treasures of their country. Whenever we go anywhere, to my despair Swamy is simply not interested in viewing the beauties of art or literature or history. When the Chinese politely asked him what he would like to see, he said he would like to examine the basement stacks of their University libraries. (Since no one else had ever asked for that, it took an order from the Governor of Nanjing to get him in there). He did enjoy viewing the pandas of Yunnan though and even today I believe the thing he most wants to see in China are the ice sculptures of Heilung Jiang.

To my delight the Chinese were not having any of Swamy's waywardness: whether he liked it or not they inexorably frog-marched him to the Great Wall, the Ming Tombs, the warriors in Xian and the bronzes of Lanchow- (Swamy had put the last on his wishlist simply because he was hoping to see the Chinese rocket facilities there; but these of course were not laid on; since anyway we had been sent to Lanchow, they took him to the museum there). As a special treat, in Urumchi they took us to see a Raj Kapoor film; but as in Egypt, Swamy would much have preferred a Bond thriller or something with Cowboys and Red Indians.

For me, Swamy's reaction when I took him to Westminster Abbey was a revelation. Steeped as I am in years of study of English history and custom, it did not strike me as odd when the Abbey doors were suddenly flung open and a glorious procession of red and gold choirboys in full throat, and waving smoking incense burners and other sacred objects, swept in headed by some equally gloriously dressed Church dignitaries. But to Swamy who had never ever studied the Anglican liturgy, it was as good as a circus. He stared open mouthed with the same sort of interest as he would have taken in a tribal dance of some remote African natives.

In the last two years I have watched our present Prime Minister on TV, thoroughly enjoying ceremonial welcomes and viewings all over the world. I cannot even begin to imagine what Swamy would do in his place; but I am positive he would not have enjoyed or even tolerated the tamasha.

For years now Swamy has criss-crossed India from meeting to meeting and seminar to seminar; he has gone to some of the most fascinating tourist spots in the world, but has shown no interest outside the venue of his lectures. When we went to the Taj Mahal, the only thing he wanted our guides to show him were the little known underground cellars where ancient Hindu sculptures are stored. (These of course are under seal; so Swamy has seen them only in photographs).

Once when we had a longish stopover in Amsterdam, I decided to use it to visit the Keukenhoff Gardens. They are quite some distance from the airport, so in my usual economical manner I meticulously worked out train and bus connections, (though even I did not opt for a bicycle connection that was on offer). It went to naught: Swamy (who in any case does not know one flower species from another or even from a weed) simply ordered a luxurious cab service, and conscientiously escorted me round all those exquisite flowerbeds and glades but without once getting out of the cab. After two hours, he announced firmly that I had had enough viewing largesse, and took me back to the hotel so he could watch TV and nap till his flight was called.

When we visited Japan, he dutifully but unenthusiastically followed me around some of the finest temples, palaces and museums in Japan; but the thing that really enchanted him, (other than the plastic and rubber replicas of food that all Japanese restaurants used to exhibit) was a penguin at the Tokyo Zoo, who had perfected a set routine: it would walk down to the water, dive in and swim across the pool, then walk once more to the other end of the pool, dive in and swim once more across the pool, and so on *ad infinitum.* After an half an hour of this I dragged Swamy away to more elevating sights. I am as fond of animals as any normal human being but I began to tire of being dragged by Swamy from zoo to zoo, which he delighted in doing.

The zoos to Swamy were the repositories of odd little animals. It was never the tiger or elephant or deer cage we would stop before; but the monkeys and kangaroos and parakeets and kookaburra ones. He would have liked to stop at the reptile cages; but I don't like snakes, human or otherwise. For years Delhi Zoo housed a Hoolock Gibbon and Swamy would unfailingly wend his way there to listen fascinated by its howls. And to exchange making faces with it. He said he did it to entertain the children; but to me it was evident that it was for his own enjoyment. Certainly, one of the first things I learnt about Swamy in the U.S., was that it had always been his dream to keep a pet monkey; and of course I vetoed that.

Of course, his most accessible love has always been dogs. My father hated dogs and so we had never had one. Swamy's family were not opposed to them, (when his doctor uncle returned to the US they offered his dog a home), but it would not have occurred to his father to actually adopt one; so Swamy got his own first dog simply by stealing it. A family friend from Bangalore stayed with them overnight, and he had brought along the puppy he had just acquired. It was impossible to separate Swamy from that puppy. He played with it the whole day; and when he heard his father quietly telling his friend that they would wait till Swamy was asleep before taking it away, he kept himself awake all night to safeguard against such a deprivation. Eventually the family friend simply presented it to Swamy.

That dog was Swamy's dearest companion. All good Tamil dogs have English names like Johnny and Tommy and Sammy; but Swamy's was a little unusual. There was nothing atypical about its name which was Winnie; the odd thing was that Swamy named it after a most unlikely hero, Winston Churchill.

So when we were back in India, of course, we got a puppy. It was a mongrel puppy, (also named Winny) that we had picked up from the dak bungalow at Bharatpur Bird Sanctuary; and a two year old Gitanjali was allowed to take it with her wrapped in Coomi's shawl. However, she quite unnecessarily promised its mother that she would return it soon; and of course she did not. After that every time we took the Rajdhani to Bombay, and the train halted at Bharatpur Station, Gitanjali would hide in the toilet just in case Winny's mother was on the platform looking out for her puppy.

Anyway Swamy brought Winny up Swamy fashion. He crammed it with calcium and vitamin tablets, so that it grew large; and he wrestled with it and encouraged it to be rowdy and contentious like himself. If he had the slightest sniffle, Swamy would be at the Government Vet's in Motibagh, where the orderlies remembered him from the days when the schoolboy Swamy used to bring the earlier Winnie there. After that we had a series of Winnys; and it was my constant complaint that as Swamy became busier and busier he had less and less time to supervise their depradations—and they did wreak depradations because any dog brought up on Swamy's regimen of calcium and vitamin tablets and wrestling was bound to be rumbuctious and a menace to the neighbourhood.

I still have a conscience problem about our last Winny. Swamy was away in the U.S. and Gitanjali was studying very hard for her IIT entrance exams and that Winny became more and more ferocious. He had managed to bite everyone—visitors and all the family members—except Gitanjali and me; and Gitanjali was becoming a nervous wreck keeping him under control. When we locked him up on the roof he howled and my neighbour, who was superstitious, complained that every time he howled she was sure that something terrible was happening to her son who was abroad. At my wits' end, I took Winny across to the Vet, (our Motibagh Vet had retired and set up practice in Greater Kailash, so he knew us all well); and asked him to put Winny down. I dared not tell Gitanjali in advance because I knew she and her father shared the same adoring feelings for all dogs; and as a punishment to myself I personally held Winny while the vet injected him….. It was the most wonderfully peaceful death I have ever imagined. Winny simply fell asleep and never woke up. Ever since I have been suggesting sodium pentothal injections as a more humane form of execution than hanging.

I also vowed we would never keep another dog. Gitanjali found it very difficult to forgive me; and for a few years after Swamy returned from the US, he too had a sad deprived look. He confided his woes to his friend N. Ram who breeds dogs; and Ram promised him a puppy which he said was so well bred that it would never give anybody any trouble at all. He was as good as his word. He gave us the most wonderfully polite and well mannered little golden retriever Egmont, (named for the Overture); and introduced us to the civilised world which is peopled by purebred golden retrievers. Since then we have had Elsa, (named for Chu's college which Delhi-ites call LSR) and Esme and Esmerelda and Evangeline and Evita and Emily and Elliki. Eventually we ran out of e-names and she-dogs and moved on to the twins Jimmy and Ludwig. Now that I am quite old, and Swamy never stops travelling we do not officially own a dog, so Swamy has shifted to playing with my daughter Chu's dogs and making them beg for Chew Sticks. But even there he is a snob. He adores her large fluffy golden Kiki; so when he is in town the chances are you will find Kiki sharing Swamy's comfortable bed; but he has nothing but sour comments to make about Chu's snappy spaniels. He says they "lack class"—the most devastating criticism Swamy can make about either man or beast.

Apart from dogs, the only other interest Swamy seems to have outside his work and study, is cricket–even though now the only cricket he actually watches is by keeping the

TV on while he studies at something else. As a kid, he had actually reached school and college team level. He will joyfully recount a story of his experience in Calcutta at the ISI, where he was captain of a team which went across the State to Khadagpur to play with the locals. The Visitors won; the Locals were visibly irate and unsportsmanlike; Swamy called all his team together and pointed out that it looked as if the losers were out for blood and so it might not be advisable to linger on for the invitation dinner. The others, all excitable self-respecting Bengalis, refused indignantly to take his advice, so a lone Swamy caught the early train back to Calcutta. The rest of the team arrived next day in a somewhat battered condition. At Harvard, (Americans are obsessed only with baseball and football), he actually managed to organise the more Anglophile faculty members in Lowell House into a cricket team. But it was not a generally known or popular sport and recruitment was thin. (Even I was pushed in somehow though I understand neither the game or its rules). So instead Swamy worked out his cricket enthusiasms by regularly driving a group of equally enthusiastic Indians to Connecticut to play against a West Indian team there. I am sorry to tell you the West Indians invariably won.

But Swamy's real moment of glory in cricket came as a Member of Parliament. There is, (or at least there used to be) an annual Lok Sabha Versus Rajya Sabha match (Swamy has played on both sides); and in their all powerful way Parliament members used to manage to commandeer the hallowed Firoz Shah Kotla grounds as their venue. Swamy, who all through his star struck childhood had dreamt of a day when he would stride across those hallowed grounds, discovered that he was actually going to be allowed to play on them. When finally Indira Gandhi handed him the Man of the Match Cup, his cup of joy overflowed. It was almost as good as winning an election.

Chapter XVIII

SWAMY DISCOVERS THE LAW

I

To go back to 1981, Swamy stayed on in the truncated Janata Party. It was a tank of crocodiles and crabs, each with his own sub-crocodiles and sub-crabs, with each person out to pull down every possible rival. (One of Swamy's more cynical jokes runs as follows: "Someone put a number of crabs into a jar. Someone else pointed out that there was no lid to the jar. The punchline is, "Oh these are Indian crabs: you don't need a lid: each crab pulls down the crab above him, so none escape".)

There were two kinds of leaders/crocodiles/crabs there in the then reduced Janata Party. The "liberal"left-wing, acceptable to the Delhi intelligentsia and parasites, included persons like Ramkrishna Hegde: the loaves and fishes of power and office were invariably considered by them to be theirs as of right: even if, as is the case in all the major political parties it is the rural seats that provide most of the votes and seats, their representatives are expected to function as backbenchers, what the RSS used to refer to as the, "persons who laid out the rugs and set up the microphones". (For example, our friend H.D. Deve Gowda with his mammoth farmer following simply could not compete with the intriguing Delhi-centric polished Hegde). The old style right wing, like Morarjibhai, were invariably treated with scorn and contumely by the left, (even today it is still fashionably correct to run down Morarjibhai); and it was inevitable that Swamy would be at home there. Meanwhile I made my home in the Law Courts and kept as far away from politicians, (and crocodiles) as I could.

II

I was truly fortunate indeed in my choice of Senior: Soli Sorabjee is a brilliant mind with unmatched knowledge of the law, literature and jazz, superb court craft, great wit and a heart of solid gold; contemporaneously with me there were three other juniors: Anu Haksar, Gopal Subramanian and Harish Salve, all brilliant and gifted minds, all of whom have since risen to the very top in the profession; but they were not above giving me, much older and slower than them, a helping hand; and there was plenty of exciting work there; but it was not long before I discovered a new and demanding client—Swamy himself.

It all started at quite a low key. Vajpayee, now heading a new and rival political party, the Bharatiya Janata Party (BJP), nevertheless found in Swamy and his hints of Vajpayee's drinking, drugging and womanising habits, a thorn in his flesh; and he applied to a fellow partyman and M.P. Ram Jethmalani to put Swamy down. Ram Jethmalani, a brilliant advocate with long experience in bringing opponents to heel by embroiling them in criminal cases, thought he knew just how to set about it. Swamy had made some slighting comment about the then Mayor of Bombay, Prabhakar Pai, something about how he was not surprised that a party like the BJP should have inducted a worthless individual like Pai, into its ranks. Well that remark was falsely embroidered and published, "buried away" of all places in the Chandigarh edition of the Indian Express as an observation by Swamy that Pai was engaged in a prostitution racket. And so Ram got Pai to file a criminal complaint of defamation against Swamy, in Bombay. It was not a particularly serious crime; but Swamy did find himself summoned as the accused in a criminal case filed in a rather lowly court, that of an Additional Presidency Magistrate in the Esplanade Courts in Bombay; and Ram's young son Mahesh as well as his gifted junior Jaisinghani were made Pai's advocates to prosecute the matter. Swamy's first thought was to find and engage a lawyer; but there Ram's contacts came in the way. He was the uncrowned king of the Esplanade criminal courts; and as soon as it got known that anyone who took on this case, would have him to contend with, Swamy found that no lawyer would appear for him.

He took advice from a relation of mine by marriage, the eminent lawyer Phiroze Vakil, who offered to challenge the complaint in the Bombay High Court on the plea that a complaint, if any, lay in Chandigarh and not in Bombay; but the High Court dismissed that observing that if even one person in Bombay had read the Chandigarh newspaper, the matter could be filed in Bombay. So the matter went back to the Additional Presidency Magistrate of the Esplanade Court.

Phiroze Vakil, an eminent High Court advocate did not practice in the lowly Esplanade Court; but he knew of Swamy's reputation as a skilled participant in Parliamentary Committees, where there was quite a lot of cross examination of witnesses so he suggested to Swamy that he argue the matter in person, promising him that before a hearing he would personally coach Swamy. So that was how it was conducted.

Once he was accepted as Defendant in Person, instead of being relegated to the place where the accused normally sat or stood, (this was the court which normally tried pickpockets and such like petty criminals, so Swamy would have sat with the pickpockets), Swamy got promoted to the advocate's Bench; and he soon settled in and began to enjoy the experience of Defendant-in-Person.

The first stage of a criminal case like this is the examination and cross examination of the Complainant, i.e. Pai in person would have to enter the witness box. We always got the matter listed for hearing on a Saturday morning. On Friday evenings Swamy and I would take the Rajdhani train from Delhi to Bombay Central, (Swamy was a Member of Parliament so he and his companion got free first class passage on the train), arrive in Bombay next morning and make our way with Swamy's devoted friend Jagdish Shetty, to the Esplanade Court and wait for the case to be called. Phiroze Vakil would have primed Swamy with some half a dozen questions he could bonafide ask Pai about his antecedents. For the first few hearings, a confident Pai managed; but as the questions cut closer and closer to the bone, uneasiness set in. Particularly as the Magistrate never gave our case more than a few minutes after which the case would be adjourned to some other Saturday, when the hapless Pai would be back in the witness box.

Apparently there was quite a lot of dirt in Pai's past; but Swamy hit real pay dirt when on an air flight sitting next to a fellow M.P., Murali Deora: Muraliji abused Pai saying he was a hypocrite who gave himself airs running a charitable medical clinic under the name and style of Dr. Prabhakar Pai. Apparently, Pai was holding himself out to be a doctor and was practicing without ever having earned a medical degree.

That was all Swamy needed. At the next hearing he got Pai to admit that he was a doctor, that he had got his medical degree from some College, "which gave its own degrees", and he was practicing medicine without any other license. To the Magistrate's horror, Pai broke down and sobbed that he needed protection because Swamy was harassing him with this case. "I never wanted to file this case: Jethmalani made me", he told the Magistrate.

I watched fascinated at the rest of the dialogue:

Magistrate: Mr. Swamy, why are you harassing this man?

Swamy: Your Honour, I did not initiate this case to harass him: I am the Accused.

Magistrate: I will work out a compromise. The Complainant will withdraw the complaint; but you must agree not to prosecute him on a charge of false and vexatious litigation.

Swamy: I will do so; I don't have time to waste on cases.

The Magistrate proceeded to dictate the withdrawal order and got it signed by both parties. He then turned to Pai's lawyer Mahesh Jethmalani and indicated that he and Swamy should shake hands. Mahesh stuck out his hand and Swamy backed away hastily: he was then in no mood to forgive the prosecution which launched his forensic career; but in retrospect he should have been grateful for that hands-on introduction to law. Swamy was launched on a new career, Litigant-in-Person—in particular as the Defendant in a whole series of defamation cases. However, one effect of the Pai trial and the devastating cross examination of that Complainant is that thereafter almost no one cared to take on Swamy in a criminal complaint of defamation. Except for one persistent complainant, (the series of Jayalalithaa attacks which stretched out over a period of more than twenty years, from 1995 till today, which I will come to soon), all the later defamation cases (and there were quite a few of these, including attempts either directly or through surrogates, by among others Vajpayee, Vijay Malhotra, Ram Jethmalani, and Ramakrishna Hegde), were civil defamation cases which could be conducted without the plaintiff having to start by entering the witness box, to be attacked by Swamy's battery of questions.

I notice that recently Union Finance Minister Arun Jaitley has chosen to file a criminal complaint of defamation against the Chief Minister of Delhi who has announced that Ram Jethmalani will be his counsel. When you consider Ram's matchless skill in cross examination, and that the criminal case must start with Jaitley being cross examined in the witness box, I am not sure that Jaitley was wise.

III

Once Ram himself filed a civil defamation suit against Swamy; it was transferred from the Delhi High Court to the Delhi District Court when the District Court's pecuniary jurisdiction was raised; so the entire Jethmalani chamber appeared before a District Judge in Tis Hazari, who was thrilled to have the King of Cross-examination appear in person as Plaintiff. Ram gamely allowed Swamy to put him through a long and rather humiliating cross-examination, because, no doubt licking his lips, he was looking forward to the moment when their roles would be reversed and Subramanian Swamy, Defendant, would be in the witness box being torn apart by Ram Jethmalani, Plaintiff.

But as Swamy will be the first to admit, he is not a redcoat British soldier of the nineteenth century, bravely facing the enemy in a terribly visible red coat. And in any case he felt Ram in cross examination had given him enough material to prove the truth of his alleged defamation. So when the time came for Swamy to produce his evidence he simply announced that he was not going to lead any evidence in his own defence, and so did not need to enter the witness box. A baffled Ram was simply unable to jeer Swamy into the witness box.

In any case, it turned out that the case had been filed without a proper cause of action: Ram could not produce any evidence at all that there had been any publication to a third person, of the alleged defamation, (Swamy had written solely to the then Prime Minister, Vajpayee, accusing Ram of FERA violations). Faced with an ignominious dismissal of suit Ram convinced the Judge that he should be allowed to withdraw his suit on "friendly" terms. A touched Judge took both parties into his chambers for a compromise. The conversation went as follows:

> Judge: Can I say that both parties agree to a mutual withdrawal of all aspersions?
> Swamy: No. I am not withdrawing my statement on Ram's violation of FERA.
> Judge: Well, can I at least say that you wish each other well.
> Swamy: No, I don't wish him well at all.
> Judge: (in desperation): Well I will draft a simple withdrawal without reference to any aspersions on either side.

And that is how it was done in Civil Suit, Ram Jethmalani Vs Subramanian Swamy. There was a later Civil Suit Ram Jethmalani Vs. Subramanian Swamy, filed in the Delhi High Court for a crore I think, which Swamy lost: he was directed to pay damages of Rs. Five lakhs. But Swamy forthwith went in Appeal. The matter was heard at great length twice over by two different benches; but it was never finally decided. In the meanwhile Ram Jethmalani made an irresistible peace offer, ("after all, Swamy, we are both likeminded people, anxious to work against corruption for the good of the country"), which Swamy accepted; so the matter was disposed of as amicably settled, though Swamy took the precaution of getting recorded in the Order that the points of law raised therein lay open to be decided in a "suitable" case. They are now good friends; to Swamy's eternal benefit and my gratitude, as Ram last year worked staunchly to keep Swamy out of jail in a hate speech matter. But that is another story.

Chapter XIX

JAYALALITHAA AND MORE DEFAMATION LITIGATION

I

Strictly speaking the Jayalalithaa and Ram Jethmalani exceptions ought not to figure in this book, because they pertain to a later period of Swamy's career; but I think it wise to use them here to illuminate what Swamy has had to face defamation-cases-wise and how he has proceeded to deal with them. I have only once met the late Jayalalithaa, four times Chief Minister of Tamil Nadu, a legend even in her lifetime; but Swamy had known her since 1984, when her mentor M.G. Ramachandran sent her to the Rajya Sabha; and he has dealt with her as both friend (they are both dog lovers and would exchange notes on their respective precious pooches) and foe; she was, I gather, extremely beautiful, extremely charming, extremely intelligent, extremely well read, and extremely charismatic, but aloof and extraordinarily lacking in ruth. (I recall another such ruthless person who became a friend whom Swamy knew well and who he said was equally lacking in the wiring that most humans have that makes them know these limits: Chaudhary Bansilal onetime Chief Minister of Haryana, who used to sit next to Swamy in the Rajya Sabha and thought to regale him with tales of who he had had beaten up, (actually Bansilal's expression was "broken his bones") and how: Swamy seems to collect and sometimes actually befriend such persons).

The temperature of Swamy's relationship with Jayalalithaa continually veered crazily from one extreme to another: it started with the friendliness of the 1980s and early 1990s, descended to the rancour of the mid 1990s, when Swamy initiated a series of successful but not conclusive prosecutions against Jayalalithaa for various acts of corruption and, AIADMK goons made violent attacks on Swamy, to the political alliance of the late 1990s, (which actually brought down two central governments) when one humourist Jug Surraiya could refer to Swamy as Jayalalithaa's "pet barracuda". Even now, with so much bad blood between them, at bottom there is in the chivalrous Swamy, a deep sympathy for the terrible upbringing that forced a truly remarkable and idealistic young girl with a scholastic bent, into the cess pool of the Tamil film world; and brutalised her.

From 1984 to 1992, their friendship commenced and continued cordially. M.G. R. passed away in December 1988 and Jayalalithaa had to fight for her political life with rivals in the AIADMK. With a grit and determination she is now famous for, she succeeded. Then in 1991, when Jayalalithaa was friendless, resourceless and out of power but with a large well organised party the AIADMK at her command and a name well known and much adulated throughout

Tamil Nadu, Swamy then a Union Minister had helped by getting the DMK Government dismissed; and this enabled Jayalalithaa to recoup to fight the 1991 State Elections, which she won. Jayalalithaaa became Chief Minister of Tamil Nadu.

After that, supremely confident of her invincibility, and encouraged by her evil genius, Sasikala, Jayalalithaa ran a tight dictatorship and had no use for friends, only slaves. Inevitably she fell out with Swamy. In May 1992, there was carried out an almost lethal acid attack on an honest I.A.S. officer, Chandralekha who had refused to endorse the SPIC deal, whereby Government largesse was made available to certain people. Swamy was horrified by the cruelty and violence against Chandralekha, and devoted several months to helping in her rehabilitation. Chandralekha, a superb administrator with a frank and independent mind and wide contacts in the Tamil Nadu bureaucracy, resigned from the I.A.S. and joined the Janata Party and was instrumental in organising it in Tamil Nadu. The result was the extreme violence and virulence of the 1993 to 1996 years.

It was during these years too that Swamy commenced the prosecution of a series of corruption cases against Jayalalithaa. I will not go in detail into these cases because they do not pertain to the period I am covering here, except to summarise the final conclusion of the most spectacular of them, the "disproportionate assets" case of 1996 wherein in 2014, (Jayalalithaa's lawyers managed to stretch it out to 18 years before the various successive Special Judges hearing the corruption case), Jayalalithaa was convicted by the Trial Court and sentenced to several years in jail and fines amounting to some Rs. 100 crores; the following year she bounced back having been acquitted in appeal by the High Court; and presently the matter has been heard and decided by the Supreme Court which has reinstated the Special Court's conviction and sentencing; but though these too belong to the later period I will delineate here, their (and Swamy's) contribution to the delineation of India's defamation laws.

Swamy had campaigned throughout Tamil Nadu against Jayalalithaa then Chief Minister of Tamil Nadu, urging her prosecution on a battery of corruption charges. Naturally Jayalalithaa was entitled to file a criminal complaint of defamation; but she did it in a way open to just a handful of persons, those designated as "public servant": she got her bureaucrat underlings to file a complaint of criminal defamation, u/S.199 of the Cr.P.C., (which deals with the criminal defamation of a public servant in respect of his conduct in the discharge of his public functions). In such a case, the complaint is filed not by the defamed person, but by the Public Prosecutor after obtaining the sanction to so prosecute, granted in accordance with S.199(2) of the Cr.P.C., by some Government functionary: in her case, the Chief Secretary, Tamil Nadu. And for the "defamed" person, the beauty of it is that he/she does not enter the witness box for cross-examination at the outset. So unlike poor Prabhakar Pai, the procedure was quite painless for Jayalalithaa.

Jayalalithaa did not stop at a single complaint: one complaint, complete with sanction granted by the Chief Secretary Tamil Nadu was filed before the Principal Sessions

Judge in Madras by the Chief Public Prosecutor; a similar complaint, also complete with sanction granted once again by the Chief Secretary Tamil Nadu about a second alleged criminal defamation, was filed by the Public Prosecutor, North Arcot, Ambedkar District, Vellore in the Court of the Principal Sessions Judge, Vellore. So Swamy would be kept busy shuttling from Court to Court, and that too in a hostile atmosphere, (the AIADMK goons are capable of any violence).

Thereafter, Swamy filed in the Madras High Court W.P.(Cr) No.6094-5/1993 challenging the vires of Sections 499 and 500 of the IPC and S. 199(2) of the Cr.P.C. as well as the aforesaid Criminal Complaints. Therein the Hon'ble Single Judge of the Madras High Court, refused the Interim Prayer for bail and other reliefs; so Swamy had to appear personally in Court.

Since evidently his personal security in jail, was at risk if he did not get bail, Swamy then filed in the Supreme Court S.L.P.(Crl) No. 10189-90/1993 challenging the refusal of bail. Therein, too, Swamy challenged the vires of Sections 499 and 500 of the IPC and Section 199(2) of the Cr.P.C.. Fortunately for Swamy, this matter happened to be pending and awaiting listing when something truly extraordinary and hair raising happened.

Predictably Swamy had been harassed and terrorized repeatedly when in answer to the summonses, he appeared in the two criminal courts. On three occasions when Swamy and his Janata Party workers appeared in the Criminal Courts in answer to the summonses in the two criminal cases, they were repeatedly attacked by goondas, (who had assembled even within the august premises of the Madras High Court) with lethal weapons such as acid bombs, stones, soda water bottles etc. There was a deliberate absence of police to control the crowd; and on one occasion Swamy was saved from the crowd only by his CRPF security force who fired on the crowd.

It so happened that on the last such occasion on 18.6.1993, I was in Madras to attend a family wedding and I accompanied Swamy to Court; and what I saw there made my blood run cold. The hostile crowd actually invaded the Court room of the Principal Sessions Judge, Chennai in the High Court premises and it was so violent that the Principal Sessions Judge dropped hearing the case and instead made us take refuge in his Chamber; and from there, along with our security and two dear friends, the Motilals we fled by back routes in the Court premises to the car and on to the airport. (Kamala Motilal had accompanied us to Court because she had never seen a Court proceedings and she thought she might find this one interesting. It more than lived up to her expectation).

Fortuitously our luggage was already in the car, (we were going from there to the wedding dinner and then catching the late night flight to Delhi) as we fled along with the Motilals to the airport. No flight other than one to Bangalore was expected to take off till late in the evening; but with the AIADMK goons and possibly the Madras Police in full cry, we could not pick and choose. We got on the plane to Bangalore which took off and then we breathed a sigh of relief.

But Jayalalithaa knew how to use the levers of power and she was not one to lightly let her prey go. To someone like my father's daughter, brought up to have faith in the Rule of law and order, what happened next was like something out of an improbable James Bond thriller (Swamy's idea of light entertainment is to watch James Bond style thrillers). Unbelievably, balked of her prey, Jayalalithaa got the Madras Airport Control Tower to recall the airplane in flight mid air, just before it entered the jurisdiction of the Bangalore Airport Control Tower. Swamy came to know this at once simply because at just the moment of recall, he was in the cockpit paying a courtesy call on the pilot. (It was the well known industrialist Mr. Vijaypat Singhania who used to pilot a plane at intervals simply to maintain his pilot license in good standing): it was announced that there was an "emergency", which necessitated the flight's recall. Why it could not have continued on and landed, in emergency mode, on the equidistant Bangalore runway, (which would have inconvenienced no one on board, all headed for Bangalore) was not explained; but from the black looks of our fellow passengers, they obviously held Swamy responsible for this.

As we were landing in Madras, we were told that the emergency chute was being opened for deplaning, that we should leave all our hand luggage behind, line up and slide down the chute and race as fast as we could across the runway to the Airport doors. As it so happened my hand baggage contained all the family jewellery brought to Madras for the wedding; but at a moment like this, one does not worry about such small things: in any case, nothing dramatic happened to the airplane and four days later the hand baggage along with our other luggage was collected in Bombay, from the plane by our dear friend Jagdish Shetty and sent back to us in Delhi with the jewellery intact.

It was pitchdark at the Madras airport, which was just as well as the police who had been alerted, failed to locate us. Swamy and I holed up in some lounge from which we phoned up Motilal, (who was fortunately still close to the airport) and asked him to find us a berth on a plane, any plane that was heading out of Madras. By great good fortune, an Air India flight from Singapore had just touched down at Madras, on its way to Delhi. Motilal got us two tickets on it, we rushed through security; and the flight proceeded uneventfully to Delhi.

It was two thirty in the night when we reached Delhi. Naturally since we were not expected at that hour, there was no car there for us; and no taxis seemed to be around. Fortunately a lady IAS officer offered us a ride home, so we were spared a walk home from the airport. Early next morning we were at the doors of the Supreme Court; we mentioned for urgent listing Swamy's fortuitously pending S.L.P.(Crl) No.10189-90/93, (challenging the vires of Sections 499 and 500 of the Indian Penal Code and S. 199(2) of the Code of Criminal Procedure as well as the aforesaid Criminal Defamation Complaints) and Chief Justice Venkatchalliah that same day issued notice and granted a stay on the lower Court proceedings.

In response thereto a few weeks later both Jayalalithaa and the State of Tamil Nadu appeared; and within a few hearings on 20.8.1993, a Bench of Chief Justice

Venkatchalliah and Justice Jeevan Reddy disposed of the matter, stating that Swamy could take up the matter in a Writ Appeal to the Madras High Court Division Bench, with a stay in the meanwhile.

In case the reader thinks, (I do make some allowance for normal and pardonable disbelief), that all I write above simply cannot have happened in a civilised state, (I myself was too scared to step into Tamil Nadu for some ten years thereafter, but of course Swamy was not so deterred), I reproduce the relevant part of the Supreme Court Order which reads with great dignity and some restraint:

> "3. The case of the petitioner, however is that in view of the hostile and acrimonious attitude that the Chief Minister has adopted towards the petitioner, he has had to face and be exposed to violent mobs in the State and that his visits to the State are fraught with danger and risk to his person and his life……
> 4. So far as the apprehensions to petitioner's safety are concerned, the Chief Minister of the State has filed personal affidavit assuring that in addition to the existing security set-up for the petitioner, all arrangements shall be made by the State to ensure the safety of the petitioner in every respect in Tamil Nadu. The State Government says that it would constitute a slur on the ability of the State if the proceedings are taken up here on grounds of the alleged insecurity of the petitioner in the State of Tamil Nadu. We place the assurance given by the Chief Minister on record. In this view of the matter there would be no justification to interfere directly by special leave…"

No further action was taken by the Bench in regard to Swamy's challenge to S.499 and 500 of the IPC,and S.199(2) of the Cr.P.C. On Swamy's plea thereon, (he had researched it very thoroughly and had a mountain of case law mostly U.S. Supreme Court judgements which he gave the judges), the Hon'ble Supreme Court stated that such a challenge would be taken up when a "fit case" came before them.

Such a fit case came up in the following year 1994, when a member of this Hon'ble Bench, J. Jeevan Reddy, while deciding the "Auto Shankar Case" reported in (1994) 6SCC632, utilized Swamy's detailed arguments bolstered by a catena of US Supreme Court judgments. Therein the Supreme Court actually accepted Swamy's argument that:

> "in the case of public officials.....the remedy of action for damages is simply not available with respect to their acts and conduct relevant to the discharge of their official duties. This is so even where the publication is based upon facts and statements which are not true, unless the official establishes that the publication was made (by the defendant) with reckless disregard for truth."

However the Hon'ble Bench further stated:

> "We may clarify we have not gone into the impact of Article 19(1)(a) read with clause (2) thereof on Sections 499 and 500 of the Indian Penal Code. That may have to await a proper case.".

It took a further 23 years for the Hon'ble Supreme Court to encounter just such a proper case to meet the standards laid down by Justice Jeevan Reddy; and then again the dramatis personae turned out to be Swamy and Jayalalithaa.

Meanwhile since Jayalalithaa and the State of Tamil Nadu proceeded with the aforesaid criminal complaints in Tamil Nadu courts, Swamy filed a fresh writ petition, W.P.(Cr) No.580 of 1993, in the Supreme Court, challenging S.499 and 500 of the IPC, and S.199(2) of the Cr.P.C. Thereupon the State Government withdrew all prosecutions initiated against Swamy; and so informed the Supreme Court, which thereupon, by its Order dated 11.3.1994, disposed of W.P.(Cr) No. 580/1993.

A year later, in 1995-1996 in a second round of vendetta, some 100 criminal cases against Swamy were filed in various courts all over Tamil Nadu by the local Public Prosecutors. In most of them it was alleged that Swamy had defamed the Chief Minister of Tamil Nadu; and in most of them criminal action had been initiated by a Sanction Order signed by the Chief Secretary of Tamil Nadu. These criminal cases included:

(1) Criminal Complaint No.1 of 1995 filed in the Sessions Court of Chengalpattu by the Public Prosecutor Chengalpattu on the charge that Swamy had criminally defamed Jayalalithaa by stating that in conspiracy with the LTTE Chief Prabhakaran, she was trying to cook up cases against him, get him arrested on these cooked up cases and then do away with him in jail;

(2) Criminal Complaint No.1 of 1996 filed in the Court of the Principal Sessions Judge at Madras by the City Public Prosecutor in regard to Swamy's press statement about an Enforcement Directorate enquiry into an aircraft deal entered into by Jayalalithaa;

(3) A criminal complaint filed by the Deputy Secretary, being PRC 51/S filed in the Court of the Judicial Magistrate at Tambaram, against him, of which I cannot remember the substance;

(4) A criminal complaint C.C. No.12 of 1994 filed before the Designated Court II, Madras, by the Trichinopoly police, in regard to an alleged terrorist conspiracy initiated by Swamy;

(5) There was also a case under the Atrocities Act, (the Act is directed against anyone who makes a slur against a person belonging to a scheduled caste) filed in the Madurai Sessions Court, in which the alleged crime was that by calling the LTTE "an international pariah," (pariah is actually a Tamil word for untouchable), Swamy had defamed persons of the scheduled castes, (this is a non-bailable offence).

In the last case (the Atrocities Act case), in a single day, posses of Tamil Nadu police arrived in Madras, Bombay, (my sister Soonu's home) and Delhi to arrest Swamy and take him away to Madurai to face trial for the (non-bailable) offence under the Atrocities Act. Swamy had to flee to Delhi, and hammer once more on the doors of the Supreme Court, where on the same day 21.4.1995, he obtained an

Order of protection from the Supreme Court in W.P.(Cr.)147/1995. For the generally restrained and conservative Supreme Court it was a remarkably comprehensive protection order: Chief Justice Ahmadi sitting with Justice Hansaria, stated:

> "Having heard Mr. Subramanian Swamy in person and having perused the nature of his grievance, we are of the opinion that the minimum relief which we can grant him is two fold in nature: (1) that the security cover to which he is entitled and which has been provided to him by the respondents shall not be withdrawn and, (2) any warrant of arrest by any Court in the State of Tamil Nadu may be executed at Madras but on execution he will be released on his executing a personal bond of Rs. 100/- for appearance….."

Till today Swamy is convinced that Chief Justice Ahmadi's order may have saved his life from the vengeance of the AIADMK goons and he honours him for this. But it was not the end of the vendetta.

Some time later, on 19.6.1995, the Judicial Magistrate, Chengalpattu dismissed the Criminal Complaint C.C. 1 of 1995, (in regard to Swamy's public statement that Jayalalithaa had colluded with the LTTE Chief Prabhakaran to attempt to imprison him on false charges). Therefrom the Complainant filed a Revision Petition; and, thereon, by his order dated 18.5.1995, the Sessions Judge, Chengalpattu allowed the Complainant's Revision Petition and remanded the matter back to the Chief Judicial Magistrate

Chengalpattu. Therein on 12.2.1996, in the restored C.C. No. 1 of 1995, the Judicial Magistrate Tambaram (Chengalpattu) dismissed Swamy's application for dispensing with his personal appearance. Thus it became necessary for Swamy, even though surrounded by his armed CRPF security guards to once again brave the hostile mob which would invariably collect at each such hearing.

A few days earlier on 6.2.1996, anticipating the aforesaid order rejecting his application for exemption from personal appearance, Swamy had filed in the Supreme Court, W.P.(Crl) No. 87 of 1996 challenging the vires of S.199(2) of the Cr.P.C. Therein he prayed that all the above cases, filed u/S.199(2) of the Cr.P.C. be not proceeded with pending a decision of the Supreme Court.

Also, on 22.2.1996, since, as had been demonstrated in the earlier cases, it was clearly unsafe for him to be personally present in Tamil Nadu criminal courts, Swamy filed in the Supreme Court, T.P.(Crl) No. 30 of 1996, praying that all the above cases be transferred for trial to some court outside Tamil Nadu. Thereafter, probably on the advice of their Senior Counsel in the Supreme Court, all the aforesaid cases were immediately withdrawn by the Respondents; and by its order dated 25.3.1996, the Supreme Court permitted Swamy to unconditionally withdraw both his Writ Petition (Cr) 87/1996 and his Transfer Petition(Cr)30/ 1996.

Thereafter, for a period of 18 years, there was a welcome lull; and no criminal defamation cases were filed against Swamy. Then on or about September 2014 we learn't from an announcement on various TV channels, that the same

Complainant Jayalalithaa, through the same official, the City Public Prosecutor Chennai, had filed yet another criminal complaint of defamation against Swamy; and the same had been done as usual with the sanction of a Secretary of the Tamil Nadu Government. The alleged crime was that in a public speech in Tamil Nadu, Swamy waxing eloquent in Tamil and citing a couple of Tamil proverbs beloved of all Tamil people, had said that giving governance into Jayalalithaa's hands was like "giving a garland to a monkey or camphor to a donkey." Eventually there were seven such complaints.

I should mention that all these recent criminal complaints appear to have been triggered by the fact that at the end of that month Jayalalithaa had been summoned to appear to judgement in a case against her of having assets far in excess of her known sources of income, which case was originally filed in the early 1990's by Swamy in the Court of the Special Judge, Chennai, under S. 13 of the Prevention of Corruption Act. In October 2015, Jayalalithaa was convicted therein; and she resigned both her seat as an M.L.A. and the Chief Ministership. She appealed, her appeal was allowed, she refought and won a seat in the Tamil Nadu Assembly; and she was back in office as Chief Minister, without a blemish on her air name. Now it was upto Swamy and the State of Karnataka to try and upset that in the Supreme Court: which they did with spectacular success. On 14-2-2017, the Hon'ble Supreme Court allowed their Appeal from the High Court acquittal of Jayalalithaa. In a judgment running into several hundred pages, wherein are laid down some resounding observations on the crying need of the hour, for the courts to act firmly and decisively against the rampant corruption prevailing in India, the Supreme Court reaffirmed the Special Judge's conviction and sentence. Jayalalithaa herself had passed away just two months earlier; but her co-conspirators have once more been jailed for four years and fined. For Swamy there was a particular satisfaction: towards the end of his arguments before the Supreme Court, in May 2016, before the Court rose for the day, one of the Hon'ble Judges asked for a promise from Swamy:

> "Promise me, Dr Swamy that you will never give up your fight against corruption".

It is a compliment that Swamy will treasure and honour all his life; and a promise he will always keep.

As far as the defamation cases, filed in 2014, after a gap of eighteen years, (he had not been idle in those years, he had quite a number of cases going in High Courts and the Supreme Court, many of them reported decisions of some moment; but there had not been any further criminal defamation matters), Swamy was once more in the Hon'ble Supreme Court, invoking its jurisdiction under Article 32 of the Constitution of India, and challenging once more the same three sections—Sections 499 and 500 of the IPC and Section 199(2) of the Cr.P.C. This time, a string of notables tagged themselves along with Swamy's matter including Rahul Gandhi and Arvind Kejriwal, (clearly the criminal defamation laws have a lot of very varied victims!). On 13.5.2016, the Hon'ble Supreme Court passed judgement in W.P. (Crl) No. 186 of 2014, in the matter of Dr. Subramanian Swamy Vs. Union of India, Ministry of Law and Others, (Jayalalithaa was there alright but as Respondent No.2).

To our disappointment, the Hon'ble Supreme Court has upheld all three impugned sections. Alas, in life one must struggle; so I guess we will have to struggle with the criminal defamation law as it stands, unaltered in its lifetime of a century and a half.

Chapter XX

MORE LAW CASES NOTABLY THE "HEGDE" YEARS

I

All these defamation cases occurred in the 1990s and the 2000s; and chronologically speaking much happened before that in Swamy's career in the law courts. But I believe there must be some system in delineating Swamy's numerous run-ins with the law, and that the criminal defamation cases should go together. Chronologically though after Prabhakar Pai's matter, in the Esplanade Court in Bombay, Swamy's next foray into the law was in the august halls of the Supreme Court in March to May 1987. And the matter started in Tamil Nadu. The Government of India was working out an arrangement whereby Kachhathivu, (a disputed island in the Palk Straits) was to be handed over to Sri Lanka. This was opposed by Tamil fishermen who had traditionally landed on Kacchathivu to dry their nets and pray at the small church of St. Anthony there. And Swamy was leading their agitation. At least he was supposed to be leading the agitation; but when he reached Madurai on his way south to the coast, the Tamil Nadu Government deciding that the matter could balloon into a law and order hot potato, more or less locked Swamy into his Madurai hotel room and would not let him proceed further south.

A furious Swamy had to return to Delhi. He proceeded to study the law and came to the conclusion that he was being denied his fundamental right, guaranteed under Article 19(1)(d) of the Constitution of India, to freely move throughout the territory of India. So he determined to file a Writ Petition in the Supreme Court.

I was not very encouraging: normally the Supreme Court expects you to exhaust all other avenues of relief by going first to the High Court. Both my friends and advisors Soli Sorabjee and Gopal Subramanian, too assured Swamy that the Supreme Court would not give him any relief. But Swamy felt he knew better, and so it turned out. The Chief Justice, Justice Venkatramaiah issued notice; and when the State of Tamil Nadu appeared protesting that Swamy was creating a law and order problem, Justice Venkatramaiah fell on them like a ton of bricks. If there was a law and order problem, he said majestically, it was the duty of the Government to give Swamy protection and enable him to exercise his fundamental right. So it was the State of Tamil Nadu that fell in line, promising all assistance to Swamy to protest on Kachhathivu.

Swamy's friend, the then Prime Minister Rajiv Gandhi, was even more helpful. An Indian naval vessel was sent to escort Swamy, who (he was after all a one time school and college swimming champion) swam pobble-fashion through the Palk Straits, reached the island, prayed at the

Catholic church of St. Anthony there, and then swam back while the Sri Lankan navy just looked on politely. It was all good publicity; unlike the pobble, Swamy lost no toes in the process; and of course he gloried in it all.

II

Then it was back to more defamation cases. The new initiator was Ramakrishna Hegde, former Chief Minister of Karnataka another great favourite of the liberal intelligentsia, who wanted to see him as Prime Minister some day. Hegde had for some time, been nursing a grudge against Swamy who had caught him out in a case which hit the headlines as the "Phone Tapping Case".

The facts are the stuff of Indian intrigue, which is second to none anywhere in the world. The ill will between Swamy and Hegde dated back to the 1977-1978 days of Janata Party rule, when Hegde, (who had spent the Emergency years in jail, and then lost the Lok Sabha elections) was jealous because Swamy was both a winner to the Lok Sabha and an Emergency hero. Hegde had been a very senior member of the Congress (O); and so in 1977, he had been made General Secretary of the Janata Party. As General Secretary of the Janata Party, Hegde attempted to curry favour with Vajpayee by talking the Janata Party President, Chandrashekar into keeping Swamy from being nominated to the Janata Party National Executive (at that time, against Vajpayee's intrigues, but with the support of Morarjibhai and Nanaji Deshmukh, Swamy had been elected by Janata Party MPs by a wide margin to a far more elevated and powerful post on the Janata Parliamentary Party Executive).

Swamy does not forget an ill turn like that. In 1984, when the Janata Party split once more, Swamy, (expelled by Chandrashekhar from the Janata Party and kept out of the BJP by Vajpayee) joined the BLD, the party of Chaudhary Charan Singh and later of his son and successor Ajit Singh. More than that, Swamy kept a promise he had made to a dying Chaudhary Charan Singh, by effecting a fresh rapprochement with Chandrashekar. Hegde was by then intriguing to replace Chandrashekar as President of the Janata Party. Swamy arranged for the BLD to merge in the Janata Party, threw the BLD support behind Chandrashekar, and got Chandrashekar's support to make Ajit Singh its President. In the process Swamy became a General Secretary of the Janata Party.

All this was a spoke in the wheels of Hegde who, already Chief Minister of Karnataka wanted also to be Janata Party President and thus the unquestioned top boss of the Janata Party. In the Byzantine labyrinth of politics in India in the late 1980's, someone tapped Ajit Singh's telephone and recorded a series of conversations between Ajit Singh and Hegde's Karnataka rival H.D. Deve Gowda. Surprisingly, it transpired that it was not the usual villain, the Congress Government at the Centre, that was doing the tapping; and it was satisfactorily proved by documents, (revealed in Parliament in an Oral Reply), that the tapping was being done, (quite legally, on the pretext of a perceived police security need) by-of all things—the Karnataka Government at the behest of its Chief Minister, Ramakrishna Hegde. Worse still, it emerged that on Hegde's instructions the telephones of 54 other persons, (including intriguingly, a few mistresses of

Hegde) were being tapped by the Karnataka police. All this came out in an oral reply in the Lok Sabha, orchestrated of course, by Swamy with a little help from Rajiv who arranged for the seven preceding Congress Party questioners to be absent when their names were called—so that the phone tapping question, (it was way down, as eighth in the List and normally would not have reached at all in Question Hour), and a Supplementary thereon could be orally replied to with all due parliamentary publicity. As Swamy put it, for the great white hope of the Liberal Left to be caught out in such a condemnable action as tapping all those phones, was "like catching a padre in a brothel". Hegde of course denied all wrong doing; but at the insistence of Biju Patnaik, and possibly to live up to the, (if you ask me impossible and only-for-public-consumption) standards of his liberal left constituency, he nobly took the responsibility on himself as the head of the Karnataka Government: he resigned as Chief Minister. The liberal left applauded this great vindication of their high standards of public morality; but that was small comfort to the defrocked Chief Minister.

Swamy then proceeded to rub salt in Hegde's wounds. Through his Gowda contacts in the Bangalore land department, Deve Gowda, already at the receiving end of Hegde's Karnataka intrigues, obtained and handed over to Swamy reams of documents on land scams in which Hegde appeared to have specialised, thereby enabling his son-in-law to corner Government land at dirt cheap price and then sell them to builders at a huge profit. From this mountain of documents, Swamy selected the two most promising and well documented, which later became notorious as the "NRI land deal" involving prime Government land in Bangalore and Mysore, practically gifted to an NRI Cooperative Society; and Swamy gave a press conference to bring that to the public notice. With Ram Jethmalani's ready help Hegde filed a defamation case against Swamy: prudently remembering the Pai fiasco, he filed a civil case (not a criminal case), claiming damages of Rs. 1 crore and a further compensation of another crore. In those far off days, a crore was a lot of money, (it would be worth about Rs. 15 crores today); and the newspapers and broadcasters gave it ample publicity. I remember two shell shocked listeners: our cook and my mother both of whom wondered aloud how Swamy was ever going to pay off an amount like that.

Swamy was not fazed, he already had all the justifying material he had collected against the day of the suit. But it never came to the point where he actually had to use it in court—in the process he had to do quite a lot of fancy legal footwork.

Because Ram Jethmalani was helping organise Hegde's suit behind the scenes, Hegde filed the suit, not in its natural setting in Karnataka, but in the Bombay High Court. For Hegde it had an additional advantage: Bombay High Court had a limit on court fees so whether you claimed damages of Rs 20 lakhs or two crores or the moon, the court fee was the same. But that choice of Hegde's gave Swamy his first victory. Swamy, by now quite comfortable in his advocate-without-benefit-of-law-degree skin, argued the matter himself in the Supreme Court, claiming his right to have the case tried in its natural forum in Bangalore. Actually, considering that he had been Chief Minister there, it is really surprising that Hegde did not himself settle on Bangalore where presumably he had clout. His own publicly announced reason was that he had nobly foreborne using his natural advantage there because it might have put his opponent at a disadvantage! But of course, most people were willing to believe Swamy's insinuation that Hegde's corruptions and pecadillos were so well known to the good citizens of Karnataka, that courts there would have given short shrift to Hegde's plea that he was at all defamed.

It was a marathon fight. Hegde, who still continued the darling possible prime ministerial candidate of the liberal left, had the voluntary services of one of the most respected names in India, that of Justice Tarkunde. But Justice Tarkunde, to his audible chagrin, lost to the non-lawyer Swamy. In a landmark judgement Subramanian Swamy Vs. Ramakrishna Hegde, [reported in (1990) 1 SCC 4], the Supreme Court used the internationally accepted principle of forum non conveniens to transfer the case from Bombay High Court to the City Civil Court Bangalore.

You may well ask: why not to the High Court in Bangalore? The answer is that in Bangalore, unlike in Bombay, all civil suits start in the District Courts, (which in Bangalore City is the City Civil Court). So Hegde was relegated to his place in the long long, (and comparatively slow) queue of matters to be heard by this Court: so there was to be no quick spectacular victory against Swamy. Worse still, Bangalore Courts do not have an upper limit on court fees so Hegde had to pay full court fees on his huge claim of two crores in damages. He paid it: but claimed that he had got the money through thousands and thousands of well wishers each of whom sent him a money order for a rupee or two.

Even after the disgorging of the huge court fee, the Suit did not get off the ground. The Union Government had appointed a sitting Judge of the Supreme Court of India, Justice Kuldip Singh, to head a Commission of Inquiry to enquire into Hegde's land scams. Poor Hegde swore blind that this was all a political plot engineered by Swamy's friend, the then Prime Minister Rajiv Gandhi. But it did not cut much ice. Justice Kuldip Singh held the inquiry, and came to the conclusion that the corruption charges against Hegde were correct. After such a finding, of course, the case of defamation did not have a leg to stand on, (one can hardly claim to be damaged in reputation if one has been adjudged guilty of such corruption), so though the suit continued on the books of the Bangalore City Civil Court, Hegde's counsel, Santosh Hegde, (who later became Supreme Court judge in the late 1990s), took good care to ensure that it did not progress: it never ever reached the evidence stage; and finally, in 1997, Justice Santosh Hegde's juniors quietly withdrew the suit. By then Ramakrishna Hegde was terminally sick.

But the case continued to haunt Hegde. In 1989 Hedge had been nominated Deputy Chairman of the Planning Commission as the appointee of the Government of V.P. Singh, (who had led the defeat of Rajiv Gandhi's Government in 1989). Like all good crocodiles, V.P. Singh, who smelt Hegde as a possible rival, appointed him only to the Planning Commission, whereas Hegde had wanted to be Deputy Prime Minister. The liberal Left balked of their deputy prime ministerial candidate, declaimed against the Kuldip Singh Commission of Enquiry. Hegde himself gave a press conference, claiming that Kuldip Singh had been "handpicked" by the earlier hostile Congress Government, and that Justice Kuldip Singh had "obliged" his appointers by his Report. A leading Editor, (of the Indian Express), Arun Shourie, wrote an editorial against Justice Kuldip Singh headed "If Shame had Survived".

And Swamy was back in business as litigant in person! He filed three Criminal Contempt Petitions against Hegde, Arun Shourie and the Indian Express. He hardly needed to: the entire Supreme Court was seething against the Shourie editorial, which had used choice expressions like "If there was any residual sense of honour or shame, the Judge having done any of it and having been found doing it, would have vacated his seat. But this is India…". So the Supreme Court also took *suo moto* notice of the contempt, while the accused contemnors demanded that they be permitted to produce truth as a defence to the charge, (at that time the Contempt law did not permit alleged contemnors to plead truth as a defence). It looked all set for a bloody battle; but that never happened.

The Hegde criminal contempt cases lingered on the Supreme Court docket for nearly a quarter of a century. By that time, (this was just a couple of years ago) Hegde had passed away and the soft-spoken Shourie was not only on the same political side as Swamy, but was looking at me reproachfully and saying mournfully," Roxna, you don't really want to see me in jail, do you?". So Swamy moved out of the case, taking the stand that once he had brought the matter to the notice of the Hon'ble Court, his duty was done and he had no further role to play. Also, the contempt law had been amended in 2006 to enable truth of the defamation to be pleaded as a defence; so the Supreme Court acquitted all parties on some technical ground.

Early in this century Hegde died. A few days before his death, he sent a friend Vijaya Mallya to meet Swamy who pleaded with him saying Hegde wanted to see him before he died. Swamy obliged. Upon seeing him, Hegde, lying in bed emaciated to the bone, clasped Swamy's hand and wept copiously. He kept saying to him, "We should not have fought at all".

As a footnote I may mention, Hegde himself never achieved his ambition to become the first Indian Prime Minister from Karnataka: his rival, the "humble farmer" Deve Gowda, who really had no ambition higher than to be Chief Minister of Karnataka, beat him in the prime ministerial sweepstakes when in 1997, he became Prime Minister of India; but that is another story outside the purview of this book.

III

Similiarly outside the purview of this book, are the next twenty-five years of litigation when Swamy achieved his full potential as Petitioner in Person—to name only the more outstanding cases there is Subramanian Swamy Vs. Union of India, (the Kachathivu matter which I have already summarised), Subramanian Swamy Vs. Post (suing the Indian Post in the Press Council), Subramanian Swamy Vs

Bhisham Narain Singh, (on the failure of the then Governor of Tamil Nadu to respond to his Application for Sanction to Prosecute Jayalalithaa), Subramanian Swamy Vs India Today, Subramanian Swamy Vs Jayalalithaa, (another prosecution) (W.P. (Crl) 942/1992), Subramanian Swamy Vs Jayalalithaa, (on the failure of the Tamil Nadu Governor to obtain the opinion of the Election Commission on Swamy's application to so disqualify Jayalalithaa for having entered into the TANSI deal, which was a contract with the State Government) (W.P.(Crl) 319/1993), Subramanian Swamy Vs Jayalalithaa (SLP 10189-90/1993), Subramanian Swamy Vs Union of India (WP(Crl) 580/1993), Subramanian Swamy Vs the Deciding Authority, (the Tamil Nadu Governor had not replied to Swamy's Application for Sanction to Prosecute Jayalalithaa), Subramanian Swamy Vs State of Tamil Nadu, (the "international pariah" epithet against the LTTE, which was treated as an atrocity against a scheduled caste person), Subramanian Swamy Vs State of Tamil Nadu (challenging Swamy's prosecution by the State of Tamil Nadu on a terrorist charge under TADA), Jayalalithaa Vs. Election Commission, (Jayalalithaa's Appeal from the Madras High Court Judgment, where Swamy wanted Jayalalithaa to be disqualified for holding an office of profit: five Judges of the Supreme Court agreed with Swamy, and Jayalalithaa resigned as Chief Minister; but the case was finally disposed off for an unusual reason:in my advocate role I had filed a defamation suit on behalf of the Chief Election Commissioner, Mr. T. N. Seshan, our old friend; and the Supreme Court held that that disqualified Seshan from hearing the case (by then two further Election

Commissioners had been appointed so the Supreme Court opined that Seshan ought not to hear the matter under the Doctrine of Neccessity), Subramanian Swamy Vs Tamil Nadu Pollution Board, Subramanian Swamy Vs Haribhaskar, (another criminal defamation case filed on Jayalalithaa's behalf by the Chief Secretary Tamil Nadu), Subramanian Swamy Vs Indian Bank (a Supreme Court Writ petition on a bank scam), Subramanian Swamy Vs P. Chidambaram (the Fairfax scam matter), Subramanian Swamy Vs Union of India, (Swamy had taken on Dhirubhai Ambani's Reliance Industries Ltd), Subramanian Swamy Vs State of Tamil Nadu, (Swamy's challenge to the State of Kerala's attempt to control the Mullaperiyar Dam on which much of Madurai District depended for water), Subramanian Swamy Vs Reliance Petrochemicals Ltd. (Swamy had taken on Dhirubhai Ambani's company Reliance Petrochemicals Ltd; and forced it to repatriate to India some billions of rupees deposited with it for the purchase of fresh shares), Subramanian Swamy Vs Union of India and Sonia Gandhi, (Swamy's attempt to bring to book Sonia Gandhi's and her Italian family's business of smuggling antique idols out of India), Subramanian Swamy Vs Union of India and Sonia Gandhi, (highlighting the receipt of a documented subsidy from the Soviet Union to Sonia Gandhi then Leader of the Opposition in the Lok Sabha), Subramanian Swamy Vs Police Superintendant Chennai, Subramanian Swamy Vs Election Commission of India and Sonia Gandhi, (challenging the Election Commission's refusal to prosecute Sonia for perjury for her obviously false statement in her Election form, that she had been "educated at Cambridge University"), Subramanian

Swamy Vs State of Tamil Nadu, (challenging Karunanidhi's remissions of the jail sentences of numerous DMK convicts), Subramanian Swamy Vs. CBI, (wherein our good friend and wonderful senior counsel Anil Divan, successfully challenged the Single Directive provision that more or less protected corrupt officers of a higher rank in all civil services from a preliminary inquiry which could be conducted only with the prior approval of the Central Government), Subramanian Swamy Vs State of Kerala and Islamic Bank, (challenging as violative of Article 14 of the Constitution of India a proposed Kerala Government order to introduce/subsidise non-interest bearing loans specifically for Muslims), Subramanian Swamy Vs Union of India, (The S Tel 2G scam), Subramanian Swamy Vs. Manmohan Singh, (challenging the then Prime Minister's failure to respond to Swamy's Application for Sanction to Prosecute A. Raja his Communications Minister), Subramanian Swamy Vs Union of India and A. Raja, (the spectacular 2G Spectrum scam which had resulted in a national loss in the range of Rs. 1.76 lakh crores; and which has resulted in the ongoing prosecution of not just Raja but also Kannimozhi and a slew of fat cat industrialists and their henchmen), Subramanian SwamyVs. State of Tamil Nadu, (challenging the Tamil Nadu Government's attempted takeover of the ancient Nataraja Temple at Chidambaram—the Supreme Court struck down the takeover), Subramanian Swamy Vs. State of Tamil Nadu, (successfully challenging the Government's decision to break through the sacred Rama Sethu the hoary causeway whereby Sri Ramachandraji and his army crossed over from India to Sri Lanka), and Subramanian Swamy Vs Union of India, (the striking down of the licenses granted in the mammoth 2G spectrum scam). Many of these are reported cases.

There are also matters still pending before various courts: Subramanian Swamy Vs Sonia Gandhi and Others, (the presently pending National Herald criminal case in the Patiala House Criminal Courts), Subramanian Swamy Vs Sonia Gandhi, (challenging in both the Supreme Court and the High Court the lengthy proceedings whereby Sonia's lawyers were keeping the prosecution from proceeding to a speedy trial of the matter pending in Patiala House Criminal Courts), Subramanian Swamy Vs Union of India, (challenging in the Delhi High Court a foreign airlines Air Asia obtaining preferential tax treatment in India to the prejudice of Indian airlines), Subramanian Swamy Vs Union of India, (challenging in the Supreme Court, a foreign airlines Etihad using its controlling interest in the Indian Company Jet Airlines to appropriate the Indian public's use of Indian airlines and Indian airports, thereby threatening the very existence of the burgeoning airport industry in India), Subramanian Swamy Vs Union of India, (the 2G spectrum scam involving Aircel Maxis).

Finally presently Swamy has been impleaded by the Supreme Court into two hugely important national matters;

(1) The appeal in the Supreme Court to decide the fate of the Ram Janmabhoomi/Babri Masjid land;
(2) (at Ram Jethmalani's behest), the tracking down and repatriation to India of some $1.5 trillion of "black money" presently stashed away abroad.

But of course, all these are outside the time period of this book.

Chapter XXI

THE FIRST EIGHTEEN MONTHS OUT OF PARLIAMENT

I

In 1984, Indira Gandhi was assassinated; and in the resultant reaction, the opposition to Congress was practically washed away in the Lok Sabha elections. Swamy, who had won twice in elections to the Lok Sabha from Bombay North East, lost badly, particularly because by then the RSS going along with Vajpayee's hostile BJP, no longer supported Swamy. The new Congress government started flexing its muscles against us straight away. It seems to have decided by starting with making an example of Swamy. We were living in a government bungalow allotted to him under Swamy's entitlement as a senior member of parliament; and the new government, after the most disgraceful of short hearings, (I appeared before an Estate Officer, and had only just opened my mouth to argue, when he told me to stop: "You will know my order when it is pasted on your door", he said.) So it was ordered that we be evicted within a month.

It was pretty shattering. Our home, in Greater Kailash

had been rented out, and it would take some time at least to get it vacated. Both girls were in school and any sudden dislocation might affect their studies. So back to the courts we had to go for some relief. This time, Swamy did not argue the matter himself, as he well might have. I was working as a junior in Soli Sorabjee's chambers; and one of my fellow juniors, Harish Salve offered his services. Even in those early days in the profession, Harish, (who is now a name to conjure with) was not the sort generally to make an appearance in a Tis Hazari court; but very kindly he did it for us, with great success. The Judge asked only one question, "How much time do you want?". We gulped and said six months; and the Judge stayed the eviction for six months. He was a very independent man: when the Government counsel rushed in to reply, protesting that until we were moved out, the newly elected M.P.s had no accommodation, he told the government counsel, "First evict the Congress people who have lost."

II

So we got a breather. We needed it. I was not making much money as a lawyer, although I had plenty of work in a blue ribbon chamber; but we were by no means down and out. The Greater Kailash house, once it was cleared by our obliging tenant would give us a roof over our head; we had a decent amount in the bank; and I had inherited quite some shares from my father; and there was some sort of a pension that Swamy, a three time Member of Parliament would get. But over the years, our standard of living had gone up; and we were now definitely a two car family with a corresponding life style. To my eternal shame I must confess I did ask Swamy, "Now how shall we make ends meet?"

Faced by my Parsi feeling for security, Swamy swung into action. A phone call to friends at Harvard, brought him the promise of a job there within a few months; and it could even be made permanent. Eventually Swamy was at Harvard for two summer schools and one college year; and that gave us the much needed financial respite. The children and I stayed on in Delhi, moving quite early into our Greater Kailash home, and a reasonable standard of living.

Meanwhile, Swamy was not just sitting around teaching courses at Harvard. Every weekend found him moving around the U.S., talking to a fascinated Indian diaspora. He also made friends with two groups: the alienated Sikh groups abroad, and the Tamil groups working for Eelam in Sri Lanka.

The connection with the Sikh groups dated back to the early nineteen eighties. Swamy was hostile to the Khalistan movement; but he does feel strongly that Hindu society owes an unrepayable debt to the Sikh community, and the Sikh gurus who had fought to safeguard Hinduism against the Mughals, and that most recently, other Sikh claims had been unjustly treated by Indira Gandhi: she had first built up Sant Jarnail Singh Bhindranwale as a counter to the Akalis; and then when he showed that he was not amenable to her control, she proceeded to vilify him. Swamy did not agree with a lot of Sant Bhindranwale's views; but he respected him as a holy man who advocated views similar to his own, where drinking and drugs were concerned (though Swamy, unlike the Sant, has never advocated crushing these with violence); and in 1982-1984, he met him several times, discussed a lot of ideas with him, and spoke up for him in his interaction with the media which was generally hostile to him. On one occasion, at Sant Bhindranwale's prompting he spoke to Indira Gandhi to suggest she meet the Sant and try to understand his view point. Indira Gandhi brushed this aside saying that she could not venture into an Akal Takht bristling with weaponry. The Sant when told this roared with laughter, pointing out that Indira Gandhi had not hesitated to embrace a Yasser Arafat who was actually carrying a pistol at that time.

Because he sensed that Swamy carried some small credibility with her, Sardar Zail Singh then President of India, asked Swamy to plead with the Prime Minister not to bring in the Army. When Swamy asked her, she denied any such intention, but enquired, "Why should I not do so?". Swamy could only point out that when a Sikh felt wounded, there were no lengths he would not go to avenge himself: he pointed out how General Dyer and Sir Michael O'Dwyer had been relentlessly pursued for years and finally assasinated.

When, the Indira Gandhi Government made the Indian Army take the terrible step of invading the Golden Temple in Amritsar, Swamy was shaken. I can recall a press interaction Swamy had that day in Bangalore. Possibly the only main line politician in India to do so, he roundly condemned the Army action, even though the entire Bangalore Press Corps savagely turned on him as a traitor.

Indeed the last time Swamy met Indira Gandhi, it was

after this, in the Parliament House corridors. She stopped him to say that, he had turned out to be right in warning her of the consequences of upsetting the Sikhs; but on Swamy's pleading that even now she could take some placatory steps, she only said "Its too late now." A few days later her prediction and Swamy's warning to her came true: it was indeed too late to save her from assassination.

Then, while in the U.S. in 1985-1986, Swamy met several of the disaffected Sikh leaders, and tried very hard to bring them back and reconcile them to India. It was a difficult task when even in India, devout Sikhs though totally committed Indians, could not reconcile to the invasion of their holiest shrine: a devastation compounded six months later by the killings in the anti-Sikh riots notably in Delhi, killings in which the most prominent perpetrators have even now not yet been brought to justice. The result is that, even today Sikhs have a warm appreciation for Swamy. One very powerful group of Sikhs, which controls a considerable vote in Canada, particularly in the western state of British Columbia, has usually been inimicable to Indian non-Sikh politicians; but when Swamy visited Vancouver last year, they made a point of honouring him in their gurudwaras. Indians in the U.K. are traditionally Labour supporters; but Swamy spoke with them for the Conservatives in last years' elections; and he received a cordial reception from Sikh voters there. Though one does not give Swamy the credit for that, it is a fact that the solid Sikh vote for Labour fractured and thus in the narrow margin results the Conservative Party benefitted: they got absolute majority in Parliament.

As to the Eelam movement, Swamy has consistently demanded devolution for the Jaffna Province; and while he was in the U.S. in 1985-1986, he spoke all over the U.S. endorsing the Sri Lankan Tamil demands for devolution. Even before the Indian Government sent the IPKF to assist the Sri Lankan Government against the LTTE, Swamy had been urging that such a force be sent. He had also offered to tour to popularise the Tamil cause in Northern India and to lobby for them in Delhi. By the time he returned to India in 1986, Swamy had become known and respected by all the Sri Lankan Tamil groups, other than Prabhakaran's LTTE. He was on the latter's hit list and ever since, (except for a short gap when Vajpayee was Prime Minister), has been on the Indian Government's Z Security List.

III

By the time Swamy was back in India, in 1986-1987, there was a third foreign group with whom Swamy had developed cordial links—the ruling clique in Pakistan, that of General Zia Ul Haq who was then attempting to bring to the World's notice the Russian invasion of Afghanistan. General Zia's contact with Swamy dated back to the days immediately after he took over power in Pakistan, and then had got tried and hanged Zulfikar Ali Bhutto on the charge of a conspiracy to murder a fellow Sindhi politician. Such murders are not so unusual in rural Sindh; but the world was shocked when trial was followed by conviction and then by the hanging of the alleged perpetrator who was a former Prime Minister. Swamy and Morarjibhai Desai were among the few politicians in India who did not condemn

General Zia's action. I remember a very friendly trip to Islamabad in 1980, followed by tours to the Afghan refugee camps in Rawalpindi and Peshawar. We were again invited in 1986 after Swamy's return from Harvard. When we returned to Delhi from that trip in early 1987, we were carrying a rather bulky present from the General, an inlaid occasional Pakistani table, which could hardly be hidden from the curious Press at the Delhi airport. One witty journalist made the Hindi headline, "General Zia gives Swamy a table; but he cannot give him a chair". But the chair did come to Swamy the following year, when he was once again elected to the Rajya Sabha from U.P.

Chapter XXII

POLITICS IN INDIA 1986 TO 1990

I

At the end of summer 1986, our family were all back in Delhi; and Swamy was ready to go into action in politics in India again. In the early 1980s thanks to Vajpayee's hostility, Swamy had become an untouchable for the BJP. Then when, shortly thereafter he began to grow wings in the Janata Party, (he actually contested against Chandrashekar for its Presidency in 1984 and when he discovered that Chandrashekar's followers had rigged the polling by closing down some of the party polling booths, he did not hesitate to publicly accuse them), a hostile Chandrashekar had expelled him for six years from the Janata Party. One person who stood up then for Swamy, was Piloo Mody a man of impeccable honesty and independence. So in 1984, when he had stood once more for the Lok Sabha seat from Bombay North East, it was on the ticket of Chaudhary Charan Singh's Bharatiya Lok Dal (BLD). Then, while Swamy was teaching at Harvard in 1986, Chaudhary Charan Singh was hospitalised in the U.S.; and Swamy had been there to support him in what to the

Chaudhary Sahib was the unfamiliar American environment. Among other things that deeply touched the Chaudhary, was the fact that Swamy had put the Chaudhary's book on agricultural economics ("India's Economic Nightmare") on the reading list of his Harvard course; and thus perhaps for the first time the ideas in it got international scholarly scrutiny. The Chaudhary introduced Swamy to his son Ajit Singh, then based in IBM in the U.S., and urged him to help Ajit find his feet in politics, which the Chaudhary wanted Ajit to enter. Both Ajit and Swamy returned to India around the same time; and when shortly thereafter, Chaudhary Charan Singh passed away, Swamy settled in comfortably among the late Chaudhary's enormous rural following, who naturally had adopted Ajit as his heir and successor. In 1988 on the BLD's strength, Swamy was back in Parliament in the Rajya Sabha as Member of Parliament from U.P.

By then, Chandrashekar's hold on the Janata Party was slipping, largely because Ramkrishna Hegde, then the Chief Minister of Karnataka, was trying to edge him out as President of the Janata Party. One fallout of this was a reconciliation of Chandrashekhar with Swamy: Chandrashekhar invited Swamy to re-join the Janata Party as General Secretary. Swamy then teamed up with Chandrashekar, and the BLD merged into the Janata Party, and with Chandrashekar's support and blessing, Ajit became the President of the Janata Party in 1988, despite Hegde's fierce opposition. The year before, V.P. Singh had left the Congress and Rajiv Gandhi. He had formed a separate Party, the Jan Morcha and had teamed up with Ramakrishna Hegde to try and capture the Janata Party. He did not succeed, because thanks to an energetic legal campaign conducted by Swamy before the Election Commission, the V.P. Singh-Hegde faction was unable to obtain either the name or the Chakra Haldar election symbol of the Janata Party. General elections to the Lok Sabha were by now imminent and the Election Commission, (under its Chief and sole Election Commissioner Shri. Peri Sastri) temporarily froze both the Janata Party name and its symbol: V.P. Singh's party, a conglomeration of four parties called the National Front, was allowed to take the name Janata Dal with the Wheel as its symbol; and Ajit's Party resumed the name of the Chaudhary's BLD and the symbol of a tractor and driver.

If you go through the press cuttings of those years, you can see that the first person to moot a possible National Front, (to consist of Janata, Lok Dal, BSP, Telegu Desam, Maneka Gandhi's Rashtriya Sanjay Manch, Congress (S) and Jan Morcha) was actually Subramanian Swamy; but there is no copyright in such ideas, and V.P. Singh happily appropriated the scheme for a National Front, and made it a success. It helped that he could command a deal for his National Front with Vajpayee's BJP, which of course Swamy never could have managed. Once again, Swamy, at loggerheads with all "respectable" Opposition leaders, who have always regarded him with suspicion, indeed contumely, was out in the cold.

In the ensuing General Elections, Rajiv Gandhi's Congress was soundly defeated largely because of the public revulsion to the Bofors scam. The Janata Dal emerged as the single largest party in the Lok Sabha, and V.P. Singh with the outside support of Vajpayee and the BJP became the Prime Minister. The Janata Party fared disastrously, even its strong unit the Karnataka Branch headed by Hegde's long time foe, H.D. Deve Gowda, lost badly. But with its Janata Dal name, (and its symbol of the Wheel) victorious, V.P. Singh lost interest in securing to himself either the Janata Party name or its Chakra Haldar symbol; and with a masterly legal exposition before the Election Commission,(this time Swamy did not argue the matter himself but fielded two top Supreme Court advocates, our friends, G.L. Sanghi and P.P. Rao), Swamy was able to secure both the Janata Party name and its Chakra Haldar symbol for the BLD. So Swamy was back in control of the Janata Party and kept it going thereafter from 1989 right upto 2013.

II

Ever since his return to India in 1986, Swamy had obtained a new friend, the Prime Minister Rajiv Gandhi. There had been a period in Indira Gandhi's later years as Prime Minister, when she had encouraged Rajiv to meet and befriend Swamy, but it had only been a small beginning. Rajiv remembered that during the Janata Party rule, when some of its members lumped Rajiv with his mother and her iniquities, and had even urged his prosecution, Swamy had stood up in Parliament and defended Rajiv; but that was all. (In fact,on one occasion when Swamy was changing flights at Nagpur, he was stopped by the pilot of the flight Rajiv Gandhi, who introduced himself and said he wanted to thank Swamy for speaking up for him). Of those days before Indira Gandhi's death, I can recall a distinctly chilly

Sonia Gandhi definitely cold and discouraging anytime Rajiv made a friendly overture to Swamy. Perhaps she remembered how he was instrumental in her losing her life insurance business in 1974. Certainly, I remember one encounter, with Sonia calling Swamy a coward who ran away from India during the Emergency; and Swamy, who has never failed to give as good as he got, saying that perhaps she was mixing him up with the Italian army whose tanks were reputed to have only reverse gears. Nevertheless, from 1986 onwards, a cordial relationship sprang up between Swamy and Rajiv. Surrounded as he was by sycophants, (as all the Nehru-Gandhis always have been) it is truly remarkable that Rajiv saw Swamy as a disinterested and patriotic well wisher, with dynamic ideas on India's economic development and its foreign policies.

Of course, Rajiv's sycophants saw to it that the rapprochement with Swamy was not 100%. I can recall one incident in the late nineteen eighties, when the planning was on for Rajiv's state visit to China. Rajiv asked Swamy whether he would like to be included in the trip; and naturally Swamy declared that he would love to come. So it was so planned, and the details were being worked out with the concurrence of Rajiv's hosts, the Chinese Government. The programme planning was fairly advanced when one day Rajiv told Swamy that he did not feel it was possible to take Swamy with him. "Next time, Swamy, we'll work it out; but it won't be possible this time." Naturally a rather bewildered Swamy fell in line.

Some years later after Rajiv had ceased to be Prime Minister, at another conversation session, Swamy brought up with him the matter of his exclusion from Rajiv's China trip; and Rajiv very honestly and frankly told him the background: apparently a Congress journalist friend of both, had come to Rajiv to warn him, "Do you realise that if you take Swamy with you, the Chinese will have ears only for him and his ideas, and you will be left out of mid centre!" So succumbing to his sycophant's promptings, Rajiv had dropped Swamy's inclusion in the China trip. That is how Congress functions!

However despite such sycophants, (they prefer to think of themselves as "loyal followers") in his later days as Prime Minister, Rajiv was often open to Swamy's ideas and views; and sometimes he even bucked his Party line for Swamy. Thus, for example when in 1987, in Hashimpura in Meerut District, some 40 Muslim youths were massacred by the UP Provincial Armed Constabulary, and the Congress Government both at the Centre and the State level pushed the matter firmly under the carpet, a horrified Swamy tried to persuade Rajiv to look into the matter. At first he failed: Congress Party interests were deeply involved in trying to hush up the matter. But Swamy persisted. Finally when all else failed Swamy undertook a fast unto death to force the Government to appoint an Inquiry Commission.

It was, for me, a horrible experience: Swamy just would not give up his fast until his demand was met: he was visibly in very very bad shape. At that point, purely out of a warm feeling for Swamy, Rajiv ordered the desired Inquiry Commission; and to my immense relief, Swamy gave up his fast. I also secured a promise from him that he would never again take on such a fast.

The Hashimpura matter is still in the courts: as late as last year, the Sessions Court unable to convict the pin-pointed PAC Constabulary, acquitted them for lack of evidence; but Swamy is still hoping to persuade the Courts that this is not a string of murders, but is in fact a genocide, which must be dealt with in terms of the international law on genocide.

The friendship with Rajiv really blossomed after Rajiv and the Congress lost the Lok Sabha elections of 1989. Of course, V.P. Singh and his ex-Janata cohorts under Hegde had no use for Swamy; but Rajiv was always ready to listen to him; and it reached the stage where they met nearly every day. Actually it would be more accurate to say that Rajiv and Swamy met nearly every night. Rajiv would phone up in the small hours to say that Vincent George was on his way to fetch Swamy; and Swamy and he would talk from 2 a.m. to 4 a.m. or thereabouts. What particularly touched Swamy was Rajiv's transparency, straight forwardness and willingness, (indeed determination) to learn particularly from his earlier mistakes. He feels keenly that had Rajiv been given a second chance, he would have made India a great Prime Minister.

III

It was not only Rajiv (and through him the Congress) that Swamy came to know well in those days in the late 1980s. He also renewed, (they had all been in the Janata Party when it was founded in 1977) and built up his friendship with the three most powerful rural satraps of the day: Chaudhary Devi Lal, Mulayam Singh Yadav and H.D. Deve

Gowda. He also broached ties with Shri Kanshi Ram, then systematically building up the Bahujan Samaj Party; and even with NTR of the Telegu Desam Party. Though they are no longer in the same political party, the personal friendships built up then were deep and abiding, and the warmth and trust with them and their successors continues to this day.

Earlier, Swamy had had his own personal fracas with Chaudhary Devi Lal: he had gone with Ajit to Biju Patnaik's house, where the Janata Party was debating whether to induct V.P. Singh who, out of the Congress and power, was anxious to join the Janata Party. Swamy opposed it: his view was that V.P. Singh was basically too imbued with the Congress culture to fit into the Janata Party. A haughty Devi Lal told Swamy that he did not understand politics. " You yourself have not earned your Rajya Sabha seat; and have merely been parachuted onto the throne", he stated. Cut to the quick, Swamy retorted in choice Haryanvi to which he is no stranger, that he regarded the Chaudhary's people as merely horses and mules, (in Hindi that comes out as "ghoday aur gadhey"), who were there to plough their fields, grow crops, and feed people like Swamy who knew how to wield the levers of power. While an appalled Ajit looked on, practically dancing with rage the old gentleman shook his fist and demanded that Swamy come outside where he would show him where he got off. Swamy retorted that he would not do so in case the Chaudhary got a heart attack from the couple of blows Swamy could administer if he chose. At which point Ajit who was watching the exchange with trepidation, suddenly saw the beaming agriculturist stick out his hand, shake Swamy's hand vigorously, and express the wish to be his friend, (What he said, again in Haryanvi, was, "You are a brave lad!"). Years later when I saw the finale of a Karan Thapar exchange with Swamy, the reach-out handshake and smile appeared familiar to what I'd heard Swamy describe of the Chaudhary encounter of 1988.

The Jat land of Haryana has its own notions of how things are done. Around that time, I had my only encounter with the Chaudhary's son Om Prakash Chautala. At that time, Chautala was the President of the Haryana Janata Party; and the Central Party had made a very large grant to him to finance elections in Haryana; and no accounts were forthcoming from him. In those days, I had taken over the rather thankless task of presenting Janata Party accounts in apple-pie order to the overseeing Election Commission, and I repeatedly reminded Swamy that the Haryana accounts had still not been given to me. I suppose Swamy did what he could to get the malingering accounts from Chautala; but finally exasperated by my persistence, he told me to go to Chautala myself and get what I could from him.

So, armed with the Election Commission Rule Book, I duly presented myself at Chautala's Shah Jahan Road bungalow. It was a duplex and the attendant downstairs politely asked me to go upstairs. I did so; to be flabberghasted to be let into an upstairs bedroom where Chautala sat along with his favourite cow, amid stacks of fodder and cowpats. It is not that I am unfamiliar with household pets: after all Swamy himself often receives visitors with his dogs at his feet; but I had never had to try and explain accounts to an audience of a rural Lord and quite such a large and unmoved pet. Perhaps that was why I was not very successful: Chautala was courteous and affable; but I got no accounts from him; and overwhelmed by this experience I had to return to a rather smug Swamy. (When, one day passing along Shah Jahan Road, I told this experience to Gitanjali, she informed me authoritatively that while cows could be made to climb upstairs, their legs were so attached that they could not descend stairs; since then I have had visions of the plight of a series of allottees of that Shah Jahan Road bungalow, who had to live there with Chautala's cow as the permanent occupant of an upstairs bedroom).

Unlike Parsis, who have a proper respect for accounting procedures, large swathes of India have not the faintest intention of honouring the Rule Book drawn up by the Government Mandarins. Another time, Swamy asked me whether I could oblige his friend, Shri Kanshi Ramji, who wanted some "legal advice"on presenting the BSP accounts to the Election Commission. Touched and anxious to help, I turned up with the inevitable Rule Book and Forms to be filled up in duplicate or triplicate. Like Chautala, Kanshi Ram too was courteous and affable, (we agreed that we both hailed from Pune where he had spent all his working life); but I could not get him to budge from his simple stand: the BSP had received no contributions at all, so there was nothing to declare; and on second thoughts, perhaps, we need not bother about filling in any pesky forms.

The friendly give and take across Party lines continued, even for example after Chaudhary Devi Lal along with most of the Janata Party, moved over to V.P. Singh, and formed the Janata Dal and the Union Government. Sometimes Swamy could not keep his antic whimsy from entering the picture. I remember when Om Prakash Chautala stood from Meham in April 1990, against Anand Singh Dangi, there was large scale violence engineered and Swamy protested vigorously holding culpable Chaudhary Devi Lal, (then V.P. Singh's Deputy Prime Minister) and V.P. Singh himself. Which did not prevent him from mooting the following story which appeared in the Illustrated Weekly of April 29th 1990,:

> "A Circus Called Politics.
> Meanwhile from Meham, Anand Singh Dangi's camp is wondering whether this time they will be able to procure a live lion for the electorate as promised by the candidate. The lion was Dangi's election symbol and he had made arrangements with a travelling circus to borrow one of their beasts for a pre-poll parade. Unfortunately Chautala quickly nipped this election gimmick in the bud by promptly arresting the circus owner. Dangi's supporters tapped all sources for another lion, with no success. One man even approached Janata MP Subramanian Swamy on the possibility of borrowing his large golden retriever, Egmont which has a slightly leonine look! Swamy demurred fearing for the safety of his pet. Devi Lal's people however, interpreted this as a sign that Swamy was on their side and thanked him profusely."

The ridiculous piece was illustrated by a photograph of Swamy and Egmont. Jayalalithaa, an avid dog-lover, (she was then a fellow Rajya Sabha member) saw the photograph and phoned him up to enquire after Egmont's well-being.

Again in June of that year, Swamy's party put up a candidate against Lalu Prasad Yadav who was contesting a by-election from Chhapra. It was a straight Rajput-Yadav contest; and eventually Laluji won only because V.P. Singh got him some small part of the Rajput vote. The counting went on into the small hours; and around midnight I was sent off post haste to the Chief Election Commissioner Shri Peri Sastri to urge him to hold up declaring the results, because, as I proved with the Election Commission's own figures, the recorded polling was 110%. (Shri Peri Sastri rejected my plea stating, "This is normal in Bihar"). Despite his having crossed swords with Swamy in this election, a few months later Laluji made a point of introducing himself to me. I was kneeling bent over a plug point in my living room trying to fix a table lamp, when a voice behind me proclaimed., "Log mujhe Lalu Yadav kehtay hay", ("People call me Lalu Yadav"). I looked up to see a cordial well known pudgy face with its pudding bowl haircut, made familiar by *Door Darshan.*

I mention these two episodes to make the point that, Chaudhary Devi Lal and Lalu Prasad Yadav were both in the rival Janata Dal; nonetheless the personal cordiality with Swamy was there: certainly neither of them suffered from the Liberal Left cum Vajpayee determination to make Swamy a non-person. Soon a group had been established, whose aim it was to destabilise the V.P. Singh government and bring it down. It required real skill in working on the numerous confronting crocodile groups in Parliament and out; but Swamy has time and again proved his ability to get people, crocodiles as well as others, together.

III

The first cracks came inevitably with Bofors: V.P. Singh had swept into power on the promise to unravel the Bofors deal, but once in power it became increasingly difficult to keep his investigators and law officers from uncovering the hand in the Bofors deal of V.P. Singh's own Commerce Minister Arun Nehru, cousin and one time confidante and Minister of Rajiv Gandhi. Indeed in December 1989, the Government had deliberately delayed proceedings in question hour in the Rajya Sabha, so that Swamy's pointed question thereon, (as to which ministers had been beneficiaries of the Bofors money) would not get answered in the allotted time. When V.P. Singh's Deputy Prime Minister Chaudhary Devi Lal voiced these allegations against Arun Nehru, V.P. Singh sacked Chaudhary Devi Lal. Inevitably this upset a large part of V.P. Singh's rural support.

Then too there was the Mandal fracas, which successfully alienated V.P. Singh's middleclass supporters. Even at its best, before alienating these two large chunks, V.P. Singh never had complete control of Parliament. No group had an outright majority in Parliament in 1989-1990; V.P. Singh's Janata Dal Government was supported from the outside by Vajpayee and the BJP, but it was not a perfect fit: V.P. Singh was cultivating the Mandal lobby which wanted special status and reservations for the Other Backward

Castes (the OBC's), while the BJP was steadily increasing its hold on the Hindutva lobby which was then dominated by the Upper Castes but which also had a favourable response from the Hindu OBCs. Swamy's announced calculation that V.P. Singh had committed an impossible total of 123.5% of reservations in Government services, was bound to make the BJP uneasy.

Matters came to a head in September 1990, when L.K. Advani started on his Rath Yatra intended to mobilise support for building a Ram Temple at Ayodhya. Advaniji had intended to drive all the way from Som Nath to Ayodhya; but the Rath Yatra never reached Ayodhya; it was stopped in early November on the Bihar border by the Lalu Yadav Janata Dal government which arrested Advaniji. In pique, the BJP withdrew its support for the V.P. Singh Government; a section of the Janata Dal including Mulayam Singh Yadav, Lalu Yadav and Chandrashekhar split from V.P. Singh, claiming to be the real Janata Dal and joined forces with Chaudhary Devi Lal's people and the rump Janata Party. (The number of Janata Dals each with a different initial continued quite bewildering. The uninitiated may well ask, "Why not combine them all?". The reason was a litigation in the Delhi High Court, where derecognition by the Speaker of certain Lok Sabha members was under challenge in terms of the Tenth Schedule to the Constitution and it hinged on different groups having left the Janata Dal at different times under different blocs. Though Swamy was not a member of any of these Janata Dals, his fine hand and legal know how was visible in the litigation).

Chapter XXIII

THE CABINET MONTHS

With the enthusiastic outside support of Rajiv's Congress M.P.s, a new Government headed by Chandrashekar was formed. Swamy who had been instrumental in bringing it about joined Chandrashekar's Cabinet with the portfolios of Commerce, Law and Justice and Company Affairs.

I

These were not his first choices. Swamy has always had ideas ahead of his time and in many and diverse spheres; but his first love, (it has always been his chosen field of expertise) has always been economics and his first choice would of course have been the Finance portfolio. But, in recent years, (with the notable exception of the Narasimha Rao years) the choice of Finance Minister has been heavily influenced by what corporate houses and even foreign financial interests want. Worse still, there has been the occasional Union Finance Minister, who ignorant of or unconcerned with fiscal policies, thinks that the purpose of a Finance Minister is to use all the financial investigation agencies under his control and direction,—the Income Tax and Excise Penal machinery, the Enforcement Directorate etc—to collect all the data he can about rivals' pecadillos and then use it to blackmail them—a facility which is helped, if that Finance Minister can also nab the portfolio of Corporate Affairs. And Swamy, besides being no crony capitalist's puppet, has nothing much that a keen F.M. can blackmail him about. In fact just before the Cabinet was formed, Seshan had arranged a meeting of Swamy with Dhirubhai Ambani of the very powerful Reliance Group. Dhirubhai who was quite thorough in his investigation of all appointments of this kind, (he even included a session with me in his vetting) obviously found Swamy not to his satisfaction; and so the Finance portfolio was given to the reliable ex-bureaucrat Yashwant Sinha who one presumes ran it much as Dhirubhai (and perhaps others of his kidney) could have liked—a fact reinforced to me, when a decade later the same reliable Sinha, (who had by then ditched Chandrashekar for Vajpayee) once more cropped up as Finance Minister, this time in a completely different and rival party, that of Vajpayee; and he lived upto the high expectations of reliability that he had aroused by introducing the "participatory note", in my humble opinion India's finest black money vehicle.

Swamy has always been a realist; and while he naturally had little use for Sinha's reliable dealings, and cannot be accused of participating in them, in 1990-1991 he saw no purpose in publicly recoiling therefrom with holy horror—especially at a time when every M.P. and every vote counted. Chandrashekhar personally commanded only about 54 Lok

Sabha M.P.s and it was Rajiv's M.P.s who kept him in power as P.M., and since Rajiv was very much in support of Swamy, and Chandrashekar tended to be indolent and out of his depth and therefore to be happy to leave things in Swamy's very capable hands, it became evident that quite often it was really Swamy who was running the Government. So much so that, in every political combination thereafter, (and the 1990s and 2000s were a time of coalitions) it has become customary to warn future leaders to beware of Swamy ("Look at the way he singlehandedly took over the Chandrashekar Government").

Certainly, as Commerce Minister one of his biggest contributions was the beginning of the dismantling of the License Raj, with a corresponding privatisation of some sectors, and the setting in place the foundations for a market economy—something which the next Government carried out more fully under Swamy's old friend Dr. Manmohan Singh.

Actually the situation arose because of Rajiv's unhappiness with the composition of the secretariat of top economic ministry bureaucrats when Chandrashekhar took over from V.P. Singh. V.P. Singh continued the appointment of most of these officials from Congress days, but he appears to have done so with the understanding that they would assist in discovering whatever dirt they could unearth against Rajiv and his last years in office. Not every top bureaucrat had my father's non-time-serving attitude; and many of these officers may have been willing to oblige. So, when the Chandrashekhar Government was formed, Swamy was entrusted with a general upheaval of economic ministries bureaucrats which he carried out. The question then arose, as to who would replace all these functionaries right at the top in the economic ministries.

At that point Swamy remembered his old friend of the Delhi School-IIT days, Professor Manmohan Singh. Manmohan Singh was then heading the South South Commission in Geneva; and it took some persuasion for him to agree to return. He was interested in a return to India; but he wanted a guarantee that his pay would be protected. When that assurance was given, he asked only one other thing: that Montek Singh Ahluwalia, (who had been shunted out in the general upheaval of Secretaries) be re-adjusted. Swamy promised both. Montek Singh for whose professional expertise Swamy had a high regard, was adjusted as Secretary in Swamy's own ministry, Commerce; and a guarded but clearly understood relationship was worked out. On any subject on the agenda Montek Singh was entrusted totally with giving a complete, frank and accurate file noting of the matter as he saw it. If Swamy disagreed with any of the conclusions, he as Minister, would over-rule it; otherwise Montek Singh's conclusions would be incorporated. The system worked remarkably well; but of course it did not last long because, as you know, Chandrashekhar's Government was of very short duration.

But during that short spell some remarkable things got done: it was discovered, (to quote Carla Hills) that in Indian economic policy matters, "after all those decades of stale Soviet ideas slavishly carried out, there now blew a breath of fresh air".

Originally after World War II, when the League of Nations was dismantled it was visualised that there would be four major institutions to replace the League: three of these the UN, the IMF and the World Bank were brought into functioning order quite rapidly; but the fourth one, an institution to deal with international trade, did not fructify easily. From 1948 to 1986, the nations temporised and dickered. Then in 1986, in Uruguay, some 108 nations hammered out the draft of a new General Agreement on Tariffs and Trade (GATT). It was a very comprehensive draft and visualised that under the new World Trade Organisation (the WTO), not just world trade in goods would be regulated, but even services (GATS), investment regulations (TRIMS) and intellectual property rights (TRIPS) would be comprehended and the WTO would be able to interfere even in domestic trade matters in certain areas. V.P. Singh as Rajiv's Commerce Minister had agreed to parts of it. A year later, yet another leftist Commerce Minister Dinesh Singh, agreed in the Geneva meet to modify India's patent law. Called the Dunkel Draft it came up for adoption in Brussels in 1990 when Swamy was Commerce Minister. But it failed to be carried out then: Swamy, an economic liberal very firmly in favour of a new economic order based on a world wide intellectual property law and a worldwide investment management order, was strongly in favour of them; but he had to contend with the strongly socialist Prime Minister and a strongly socialist upper bureaucracy in the Commerce Ministry. Neither would budge; so Swamy was frustrated: he did what he could by shipping off the more socialist-minded bureaucrats from

Commerce to Finance, (where they would find a more congenial home with a Finance Minister keen on polishing his socialist credentials).

Eventually Swamy managed to make his point, not in December 1990 when he was actually Commerce Minister; but in December 1995, when a wonderfully pragmatic Prime Minister and Commerce Minister actually listened to him and both TRIPS and TRIMS were adopted.

I took pains to understand the situation in Swamy's own words, in an article he wrote a year later. Much of the Indian agreement thereon was determined under Swamy's ministership: one small example of the give and take that Swamy worked out to India's advantage can illustrate this: the U.S. agreed to remove the textile quotas then prevailing against India; and India supported the US opposition to the agriculture quota system which the European countries had insisted on but which was unfavourably viewed in the U.S. Except for some outstanding labour issues, and the aforesaid TRIPS and TRIMS the trade reforms program of the WTO was adopted by the Union Cabinet on March 11 1991—the last day of the functioning of the Chandrashekhar Government, (after that it became merely a caretaker government without the power to take such a far reaching decision).

Swamy also utilised his very short spell in office to get worked out the bare bones of a new and radical economic dispensation for India. When in the next government, the far sighted and pragmatic P.V. Narasimha Rao saw these blueprints, he decided to adopt them and entrusted Manmohan Singh, as Finance Minister, to execute them.

As every student of the free market revolution in the Indian economy knows, it was a great success; whether it would have reached even greater success had Swamy been in total charge can never be known, and I am not the knowledgeable and unbiased person to speak on the subject. Narasimha Rao had wanted Swamy to take over this work; but one condition was a sticking point: Swamy must join the Congress Party, and that Swamy refused to do. It was his own independent decision but he was bolstered in this decision by his defacto guru, Sri Chandrashekharendra Saraswati, the Shankaracharya of Kanchi Kamakoti Mutt, known to his devotees as Paramacharya.

So instead of joining the Union Cabinet, under Narasimha Rao, Swamy was appointed as Chairman Commission on Labour Standards and International Trade, Ministry of Commerce, with Cabinet rank, which enabled him to be present at Cabinet meetings to discuss and decide on trade related issues. Narasimha Rao himself was readily accessible to Swamy and ever ready to consider his advice so, I suggest, Swamy's views tended to prevail.

To revert to the Chandrashekar months in office, Manmohan Singh was appointed Economic Advisor to the Government of India with Cabinet rank; so he attended all relevant Cabinet meetings and was in the knowledge of all the economic facts he required to function effectively, as Economic Advisor. (It was only after Chandrashekhar's Government became a caretaker one that Manmohan Singh relinquished this post; and thereafter until the new elected Government of Narasimha Rao was in place, Manmohan Singh functioned only as UGC Chairman).

Among the non-economic related matters that Swamy rammed through which were long remembered by his opponents, was the dismissal in January 1991 of the DMK Government: it was proved to have deep ties with the LTTE, which had been building up its armoury and infrastructure within Tamil Nadu. At that time, Jayalalithaa in the rival AIADMK was grateful; indeed she benefitted because she won resoundingly in the ensuing State elections to the Tamil Nadu Assembly, and she formed the next State Government. (The account of her criminal cases against Swamy and their warfare over her corruptions which I have sketched earlier, came at a later date from 1993 onwards). And Swamy might have contested the 1991 Lok Sabha elections from Tamil Nadu with her goodwill-only his Rajya Sabha term extended till 1994, and someone had to run the Government while most ministers were out campaigning; so he did not contest at all.

Another coup that Swamy achieved is regarding obtaining US support for a bailout of two billion dollars, from the IMF, (without any conditions which was unprecedented)—which loan of $ 2 billion in 1991 prices [$10 billion today] solved the hovering Indian foreign exchange crisis. India desperately needed this money if it was not to default on its earlier loan repayment commitments. The US was then in the throes of the first Gulf War; and it sought any sort of assistance especially in refuelling its planes flying in from the Philippines. For India, it was not at all an easy option, because several decades of a conservative pro-Arab policy had hardened and these were supported by Rajiv's Congress, which after all was what kept

Chandrashekhar's government in office. Nevertheless Swamy was able to persuade the Prime Minister to grant US planes refuelling facilities in India, to support the US demand that Iraq vacate Kuwait and condemn attacks on Israel. The persuasion paid off: in return the US swung IMF support for India's balance of payments.

At that time perhaps the closest Swamy came to a break with Yashwant Sinha was over Sinha's manipulation –much publicised in the media but never really analysed –to hypothecate India's gold reserves to the British banks. Contrary to what was fed to the public, and has since become the popular perception, there was really no pressing need to have carried out the hypothecation: since as I have just pointed out, India's balance of payments had ceased to be a problem because by then Swamy had arranged for the two billion dollar loan from the World Bank. But Sinha carried it out very quietly and without even bringing it to the notice of the Cabinet, more especially of the Commerce Ministry which was mandatory. It was done by a simple executive order, and enabled someone, possibly in the Reserve Bank, to earn a commission from the British banks for obscure purposes which is yet to be probed formally. When Swamy learned of the hypothecation and spoke to Sinha, objecting, Sinha haughtily brushed aside his objections by claiming that Swamy had no business and no jurisdiction over a simple Finance Ministry executive order. Swamy contends, that Sinha was wrong on two counts. In the first place, a decision fraught with such political consequences ought necessarily to have been brought to the notice of the Cabinet. Also under the then prevailing Import Export Regime, not even a pin could be exported out of India without Commerce Ministry clearance, and that had not been obtained for this huge gold export: indeed Sinha could have been made criminally liable for such an export, and Swamy was in the mood to have applied such screws on Sinha. His problem was that the Prime Minister, who wanted peace on this matter, (as indeed he was temperamentally so inclined on all other matters), persuaded Swamy to leave the file with him lying dormant. Swamy's stand against Sinha's proposed hypothecation and export of the gold without Commerce Ministry sanction, as being a criminal offence was however recorded; Swamy had no further option beyond making a stiff protest note which is still there in the files but unknown to, (or at least, ignored by) the public at large and Sinha's journalist apologists. The gold itself was physically shipped out by the next Government; but the ground work was that of Sinha; and the money, less commission, that thereby filled the Indian coffers, was later diverted to new requirements, which were presented as "pressing".

II

As to Swamy's other portfolios Law and Justice and Company Affairs, as far as the Justice portfolio was concerned, Swamy must have been the least interfering of Ministers. He is, I believe, the first and only holder of this portfolio, who does not have a law degree and has never practiced; so unlike other Law Ministers, he had no interest at all in stuffing the Benches with his likeminded. He had a simple rule: if the Chief Justice (after checking with

Intelligence sources) found a person fit for elevation, that was good enough for Swamy; and he routinely endorsed all the names suggested by the Judiciary. It was for me, a very satisfying aspect of Swamy's term as minister: one thing which all of us sincere advocates have looked on with foreboding is the systematic attempt, (particularly since the Indira Gandhi years) of politicians with a legal background, to build up a "committed judiciary" –to fill up the Benches, (or worse, even the Court Registries) with persons who they can later influence, whether it is for personal reasons or political calculations.

Swamy with his deep reverence for the Judiciary could never be a party to such a program. In even small ways he felt it was his duty to enhance the prestige and dignity of the Judiciary at all levels. He was, for instance, horrified when a file was put up before him to, "consider" the grant of permission to travel abroad to a legal conference, on behalf of Justice Fatima Beevi, the first woman appointee to the Supreme Court of India. Apparently, for such a trip, a judge of her eminence was expected to get the permission of some lowly Government administrator like a Joint Secretary! An angry Swamy had the rule changed so that such a permission for such an eminent Judge can no longer be in the purview of administrative flunkies.

During his tenure as Law Minister in India, there was decided in the British Court of Appeal, one very interesting case which Swamy quickly realised could have far flung ramifications in India. In 1976, an ancient Chola bronze idol of Natraja had been dug up by a farmer in a Tamil Nadu village from an old disused temple in the village of

Pathur. It had passed from hand to hand through a series of antique smugglers; and had ended up in 1986, owned by a corporation belonging to John Paul Getty of Getty Oil fame. While it was on its way to the Getty museum in California, our Indian High Commission in London learnt of its stop-over in London at the British Museum; and they were actually fortunate enough to succeed in blocking its onward journey and to lay claim to it through the British courts. Getty's people fought it tooth and nail through the entire legal system of Britain; but they lost before the Single Judge and before the High Court. It was during Swamy's brief tenure as Law Minister, that the British Court of Appeal decided the matter of Bumper Corporation Vs. the Commissioner of the Metropolitan Police, in favour of the Indian claim to the Natraja, on behalf of the State of Tamil Nadu. It is a judgment reported in 1991. 4All ER 638.

Swamy was delighted by the Court's reasoning; for the noble Lords actually held that once a Hindu temple had been erected and the pran prathishta ceremony had been performed there on the idol thereof, then the God had entered into the idol into which life had been breathed; and He and He alone had become the owner for all time to come, of the temple, its lands and its other possessions; and that its priests and administrators were merely trustees of the true owner, the God. Also that even if the temple itself became derelict and disused, the God continued to be its legal owner and the State could claim its property as trustee on behalf of the legal owner, who is the God. Accordingly the Court's held that the State of Tamil Nadu had *locus* to sue on behalf of the God as His trustee, that the Natraja idol belonged to the God—indeed, it was the God himself-and it decreed that the idol should be handed over to the State of Tamil Nadu for transmission to India. Thereafter the House of Lords refused leave to appeal.

An overwhelmed Swamy had the privilege of overseeing arrangements for the return of the Nataraja; which is now in its original home in Pathur. But that was only the beginning: Swamy was farsighted enough to realise that the reasoning in the British Judgment could be the way out of the vexed situation prevailing at the Ram-Janmabhoomi-Babri Masjid site in Ayodhya. For devout Hindus, it is an article of faith that the (then existing) Babri Masjid was built on the site of the birthplace of Shri Ramchandra ji; that for centuries a temple dedicated to Shri Ramchandra ji, in his avatar as Ram Lala, had stood on that spot; and that in the sixteenth century during Babar's reign, the temple belonging to Ram Lala had been demolished and the Babri Masjid had been built on the spot. So it has always been the ardent Hindu desire to reclaim the spot and get a temple rebuilt there, dedicated to its true owner the God.

To Swamy, the Bumper Corporation ruling looked like a way out. He was fortunate enough to discuss the matter with a group of erudite and open minded Muslim leaders and divines, most notably his friend Syed Shahbuddin. They all agreed that no mosque could ever be built on the remains of a holy building of another faith; and they felt that if it could be proved to their satisfaction that indeed there was a temple underlying the Babri Masjid, then it would be incumbent on the Muslim community and more particularly the Mosque's Shia Mutawali, to hand the building back to its true owners.

The Prime Minister too was enthusiastic about following this up; but it is India's tragedy that such a reasonable solution was never allowed to fructify during the short Chandrashekhar government. After it fell, the matter was dropped; and in the succeeding Narasimha Rao dispensation, the campaign for the temple restoration became an ugly political tool in the hands of Vajpayee's BJP. The history of the violent demolition of the Babri Masjid, the lawsuit for the possession of the site, the success in the Lucknow High Court of the Hindu claim are too well known to be repeated here. The matter is still awaiting resolution in the Supreme Court; and Swamy feels that now in 2017, after decades of mistrust and violence and bloodshed, perhaps this year, the matter may begin to be resolved along the lines Shahbuddin and he had tried to work out in 1991.

The implications elsewhere of the Bumper Corporation judgment are manifold. For example, presently Swamy is corresponding, (not very successfully so far) with the British Museum, which holds what may be the idol of the Dhar Saraswati—also known as the Vagdevi Saraswati— installed by Raja Vikram at Ujjain.

III

I should stress that I did not participate in the slightest in all this: Swamy can be very conscientious about his oath of secrecy; and what I write above is picked up from newspaper cuttings of which I have maintained a file since we returned to India in 1968. Personally what I most recall of those days is a crying shortage of grand saris: nothing in my previous existence had prepared me for quite so many grand receptions and dinners with quite so many dignitaries. Also though Swamy did travel abroad we decided that I should make a practice not to accompany him on these visits, which earlier I used to do.

I also discovered that the Press had some very traditional ideas of what a Minister's wife—presumably a "society lady" –should be like. I can recall one totally untruthful piece which appeared in a glamour magazine, in which I was featured as (of all things!) "Ghar Ki Rani", (that is to say the very domestic Lady of the House). I recall being asked what were Swamy's favourite dishes: I truthfully said I did not know; so the magazine writer very kindly wrote out some recipe or other and attributed it to me. The writer also very kindly invented things for me to say and credited me with some very traditional, "Ghar ki Rani" views and attitudes which even now make me wriggle with embarrassment. Since then I am wary of giving interviews to the media!

Chandrashekar's was not a long lived Government. On the one hand Chandrashekar though indolent, (I believe Rajiv referred to it as a "darbari culture") was a proud Rajput who did not care for the Congress continually breathing down his neck. On the other hand, Congress leaders felt that Chandrashekar was there only on their sufferance and that as soon as feasible, the Chandrashekar Government should go and Congress be back in the saddle. Finally there were the V.P. Singh-Vajpayee –left wing cohorts who simply detested

Swamy being one of the the senior most Ministers and awesomely effective: I suspect that they might even have gone along with a Swamy-less Chandrashekar Government.

By early March 1991, Rajiv withdrew Congress support to the Chandrashekar Government; Chandrashekhar sent his resignation in to the President on March 6; the Lok Sabha was dissolved on March 14 and Lok Sabha general elections were scheduled for May-June 1991. Swamy torn between his love for Rajiv, his suspicion of the Congress crocodiles, and the intransigiance of the Prime Minister's clique, (Kamal Morarka, the Minister who ran the PMO openly attacked Swamy), did not personally contest the elections, (his Rajya Sabha term was to continue till 1994), and he continued to function in the lame duck Chandrashekar Government. However Chandrashekhar's Party, till then called the Janata Dal (S), fought the elections on the name and symbol of Swamy's Janata Party. Midway through the polling schedule, to Swamy's terrible distress, Rajiv was assassinated; and thereafter, the Congress once more emerged as the largest party; and with the support of the rather malleable members of the tribal Jharkhand Mukti Morcha, P.V. Narasimha Rao, (a wonderfully wise and experienced man who had been and continued to be Swamy's friend and to utilise his expertise and ideas) became the Prime Minister. Politics in India was about to undergo a sea change, which took it from the earlier straight jacketed "License Raj" to a free market economy, (something which Swamy had been urging since the 1960s), and also into the "dharma" of coalition politics. Here was a whole new ball game for Swamy.